Meeting People: It's Not a Game
Your Path to Genuine Connections thru Bempathy®

By Jill Robin Payne, MA, LPC-S, LCDC

Edited by Roger Mensink
This cover has been designed using assets from Freepik.com
Cover Design by Jeremy Taylor
Interior Design by Cyndie Dahlberg

Publishing and Media Inquiries:

6C Press
PO BOX 270563
Houston, TX 77277

ISBN: 978-1-961613-00-3 (paper book)
ISBN: 978-1-961613-01-0 (eBook)

Printed in the United States.

Houston, TX
First Edition

Dedication

To my parents Naomi and Bernard Zeavin, my son Taylor, and my brothers Jerry, Spencer and Brad. Most importantly, to my beloved husband Byron for being my best friend.

Contents

Introduction

Are you seeking a friend, partner, or love? Have you ever wondered why so many people feel lonely, unhappy, and dissatisfied with their current situation or what they possess? This book offers 'positive support' to assist you in connecting with others genuinely and creating a fulfilling life. By incorporating the strategies and techniques into your life, you will effortlessly progress toward the goal of finding your special someone in four simple steps, all while having a BALL! What an incredible concept. These four easy steps are collectively known as BALL, an acronym (which will be explained later in this book) designed to simplify your learning and enjoyment of the relationship process.

Since COVID-19, a 'new normal' has impacted both the dating and 'meeting people' scene creating a need for new social strategies. These techniques, which have been implemented in my practice, are straightforward and have demonstrated success for numerous individuals. This concept is referred to as Bempathy, a revolutionary approach that combines banter with empathy to build and nurture harmonious, reciprocal relationships.

Interviews spanning over 30 years with more than 5,000 clients using Bempathy in counseling at pain clinics, behavioral hospitals, and private practice showed significant improvements in clients' relationships and emotional well-being, helping them achieve their goals. Feedback highlighted various benefits, including understanding their priorities and values, finding suitable partners, setting boundaries, avoiding mistakes, and managing emotions. Clients found the process enjoyable, with a positive impact on their lives. Bempathy fostered better self-understanding, supportive coaching, a sense of care, clarity in personal issues, and enhanced relationship awareness. The approach led to sustainable, healthy partnerships and encouraged positive affirmations. Counseling was gentle, patient, empathetic, and nudged clients towards accountability. (This is qualitative research).

This book is for women and men who want short, simple fundamentals to help them navigate through a world inundated with technology to meet their mate or a friend.

This book is about 1) How to meet that special someone or friend, and 2) About what to do after you meet that special someone. If you want to know how to attract what you want and keep what you get, then continue reading. You may find out that the ones you haven't kept, you haven't kept for a reason.

CHAPTER 1

Friendship - Dating: Something to Think About

There are many books that teach people how to find and get their mate or friend. The question is: Can you get them the way you want them? Just "getting" them is only the first step. Think of Cinderella. At the end of the movie, when they finally get together and it says "the end," that's really "the beginning." We never really find out what kind of a prince charming and princess they will be. Once you meet, the first few months of dating is the honeymoon phase. You know the feeling—when all is good and everything they say is awesome. Then reality begins to hit. It hits some people more and sooner than others. There is a pattern in dating, illustrating if it will be successful or not. If people have dated for one month, they will probably make it to three; if they make it to the third month, then they will probably make it to six; and if they make it to six months with smooth sailing, then they will usually go all the way. Now at around one to six months there may start to be some discussions, arguments or disagreements. That is okay. However, I do recommend that if the fights are too frequent for you or if the way you fight causes you severe pain (physical or emotional), then it may be beneficial to see a professional counselor for an adjustment or alignment. It is up to you to decide what you want to live with and what is working for you. We are talking about a tune up, prevention, nothing more than that.

If you just bought a Mercedes, wouldn't you take it in for a tune-up, especially if it were running a little rough? The same goes for relationships, whether in a marriage or not. It doesn't hurt to get a third opinion, especially in this world of fast-paced communication. (That is if you call "texting" communicating. Technology and how it is affecting the relationship process will be discussed later in this book.)

There are no fairy tale relationships. It is important to note that *all* relationships have issues. Therefore, when you finally meet that special someone and have had a blissful six months of dating and then have a fight, take a moment to realize that relationships are a 100 percent give and take from both parties. In other words, you aren't bringing half of yourself to the table. You are bringing your whole body and soul. If you get 80 percent of what you want in a mate, you are doing great. In other words, the 20 percent hopefully is what you can live without.

This is important to know because with internet dating, new apps, Facebook, instant messaging, playing games in chat rooms, etc., there are so many people to choose from that it makes it difficult to stay with just one. Staying with that special person and taking the time to see their beauty is important if you are looking for a committed relationship. Too many choices for men and women are like being in a candy store full of your favorite candy, one more enticing than the other. All of this at your fingertips with just one click. So keep in mind what you are looking for. Remember no one is perfect.☺

We can't get everyone we want because everyone can't get us.

The inspiration for this book began over 30 years ago after all my friends started to ask me for advice on relationships. Giving advice came easy to me. Remember, I am a woman. Of course, I was also going to graduate school and majoring in psychology at the time. My friends kept saying, "Jill, you need to write all this down to help people find their loves." You know how people are always rushing here and there? Well, I was no different. I was a single parent, working full time and putting myself through graduate school. I didn't have the time, or just couldn't make the time, to write a book. I would rather spend my spare time dating, exercising and being with my son. Today my son is 32, has a girlfriend and is a resident (Family Practice). So now I have the time.

What I am saying is that my excuses for not having the time for writing my long overdue book ran out. So here it is! The question is: Is it time for you to read this book, or are you making excuses like I did for the past 30 years? I believe the time is now. He or she is waiting for you to ask, to believe and to receive the fun of meeting him, her or them. By "him or her" I mean the perfect person for you.

The many self-help books out there all make sense. However, some seem to complicate relationships more than necessary. They can be time-consuming. In contrast, with this book, you don't have to read the entire thing to derive benefits from it. Furthermore, the techniques it offers can help people discover and cultivate both friendships and romantic relationships.

I am like the rest of the nation and want things done yesterday, especially with all the fast-paced technology we are using. So here is your yesterday book with a speedy guide to happier relationships.

You've heard "Life is a game, and it's all how you play it." I believe "Life is a ball; it just depends on how high you want to bounce it." When I think of games I think of people not being themselves. If you are not yourself, then you might meet someone else who is also not themselves. Think of the "law of attraction." We attract who we are. There may be some exceptions, but, basically, if we are emotionally unavailable we will probably attract the same.

One problem when people are searching for that special someone is, "Who are you?" Yes, that's right. Do you know who you are? I am not talking about your roles such as mom, dad, employee, doctor, lawyer or Indian chief. What I am talking about is what makes you tick, what turns you on, what motivates you. Most importantly, when you play you need to be yourself (of course in the best light). It is also important to remember that there is nothing wrong with you. You are not broken. You may just need to increase awareness of who you are and how that affects your situation. You may need to increase mindfulness of what is going on in your world—your patterns, habits and attractions. And you may need to increase awareness of your authentic and genuine self while keeping your independence. You are a beautiful person looking for another beautiful person to match your beauty! Sounds good, doesn't it? This is *authenticity* and *autonomy*!

All that we are is the result of what we have thought.

Buddha 563 BC to 483 BC

Being yourself doesn't mean telling all when you first meet someone. It doesn't mean giving your opinion on every little thing or dropping everything for that special someone. Whatever happened to the mystery?!!! Keep intrigue alive. If you had cheesecake every day, it would get boring and you would soon lose interest in it. You might even get sick to your stomach at the sight of cheesecake.☺ Yes, think of yourself as a slice of New York cheesecake—tasty, yummy and something that needs to be savored! Even you need variety! Think of "supply and demand."

We live in the good ol' USA where we get most everything we want when we ask. So it is understandable that when it comes to relationships or getting that special someone we want it *yesterday*! It's important to remember not to force or push anything. Remember, if you push too hard you might fall hard and the other person might fall off the cliff, so to speak. I have talked to many people who aren't even aware of their pushing! That's where empathizing with your environment, yourself and others comes into play.

Think of a relationship as a puzzle. What happens when we rush to finish a puzzle and start forcing a wrong piece into the puzzle? It gets stuck, or it may bend the other pieces. Either way, it doesn't fit. Ask yourself, "What happens when we try to fit people into our lives who aren't suitable?" You got it. Unhappiness, constant arguing, and possibly divorce.

When love is in the air, self-awareness and autonomy are sometimes forgotten. Your hormones are going everywhere, along with your mind. You've heard of being "crazy in love"? This is when we write their name down a dozen times, call them all the time and become consumed with them. Wrong! This is when you need to do the ABCDs. Not the ones from school, these ABCDs are an acronym described later in this book that will help you to date or to improve your relationships. By doing these steps you will distract yourself and most likely stay in a rational state of mind. Rationality goes out the window when your hormones are raging.

That euphoric feeling is fabulous, floating and energetic. You have butterflies and may not want to eat (my favorite part). All these feelings are so wonderful, but what happens if you start to feel euphoric after going out with that person only once? That's right. You forget about your boundaries and your autonomy. All you want is to be with that person. It may feel like heaven, but we need to stay on earth.

Read on to have "Relationship Success" today!

CHAPTER 2

Genuine Relationships with Bempathy

Bempathy is a unique approach to communication and social skills, combining banter with empathy to build and maintain harmonious relationships, both in private and social interactions. It is an interactive communication style and skill, a way of relating with people and developing authentic relationships through easy enjoyable conversation using all your senses. It is a casual and comfortable way to meet your special someone or a friend giving you limitless prospects. It has six elements which are the 6 C's. They are:

1. Communication — The ability to send and receive information that another person will understand; the ability to send and receive information to oneself.
2. Commonality — Two or more people who share the same or similar characteristics, interests, or experiences on such subjects as people, places, or things.
3. Connectedness — A feeling of fitting in or being linked with self or one or more people.
4. Comfortability — The ability to feel comfortable in a situation and/or with self; feeling physically and/or emotionally at ease; freedom from emotional or physical pain.
5. Control — The ability to perceive power, exercise limits, or have a guiding influence over situations and self.
6. Commitment — The state of being dedicated or loyal to self, something, or someone.

All the above can produce congruent conversation, however, using one or two, or any combination thereof, can create even more successful communication. To create an outcome we want we need to be congruent in our communication otherwise there is a disconnect between the sender and the receiver. How can we communicate with others if there is a disconnect? This causes us to have discomfort, resulting in negative feelings and negative communication with others in our world.

The dating process can be scary and uncomfortable not knowing where to go to meet someone or being with somebody you like and not knowing what to say or how to act. Bempathy creates a reciprocal situation of bantering back and forth finding commonality by empathizing through listening and hearing the other persons wants, values and beliefs. People that use this technique are called Bempathizers.

Bempathizers are sincere and recognize how to build a genuine relationship with another individual. Bempathizers acknowledge three distinct personality types in the world that influence their giving and receiving behavior: leaders, followers, and compromisers. They understand that actions create reactions, and because they are at the center of their world, they recognize that their actions will impact how their world responds to them. Therefore, they know about the importance of timing and position of when and where to bring up certain topics and when to keep quiet. They empathize by engaging in banter and pleasing talk getting the conversation to flow. It's a practice they use regularly to meet their needs and desires.

In the upcoming chapters, you will discover the significance of utilizing Bempathy to both find and maintain your partner or friends. Bempathy makes it fun by empathizing with yourself and others so that you will know what to say and do. Of course sometimes we all get nervous however, the techniques you will learn will turn most of those awkward situations into a more comfortable scene by finding commonality or merely having a readymade elevator pitch.

Step into a captivating journey with a "Bempathy Tip" at the end of each chapter. Whenever you spot one of the 6 C's being used underline it in vibrant red. As you read unlock the power to enhance your life situations. Enjoy the process of Bempathizing and nurture profound connections with that special someone or make new, lasting friendships. Let this delightful adventure guide you towards a fulfilling life of understanding and boundless joy! Get ready to unleash the potential within you and embrace the magic of Bempathy.

CHAPTER 3

Relationship Success Begins Today

Are you asking yourself:

Where is that perfect person for me?

- How do I build my self-confidence?
- How do I behave when we first meet?
- How do I get to know that special someone?
- How do I know if they are the one for me?
- How do I know the difference between love and lust?
- How do I know when a person is a friend?
- How do I overcome the fear of commitment?

The truth is that he, she, or they are out there for you, waiting just for you. This book is going to take you on a journey to happiness and contentment and help guide you to that special someone. You will find that your life will improve in all aspects—family, friends, work, health . . . You have been a success so far and may have found a bump in the road. Sometimes "us people" get stuck on that bump. Some go over it and continue to find the same kind of bumps, and some choose to go a different route. If you are reading this book, you are the latter.

Congratulations on your choice to take a different path. I had someone tell me this morning that the difference between my coaching and all the other books she had read is that I left it up to her to decide what works best for her. There is nothing wrong with the general public, and no one needs to be fixed. You are not a car, although you may need "an adjustment." You don't need to change who you are. There *is* someone for everybody. As a matter a fact, there is more than just one person for everybody. That means that if you are a widow, widower, divorcee, person never married or have just ended a relationship, there is another person out there waiting to meet you. Ah hah! Usually you read self-help books, and they tell you, "Hey, you are doing it all wrong. You need to change!!" I don't know about you, but if someone told me that I needed to change being me, then I probably would not hang around that person.

Think of yourself as a classic 1968 Camaro that may have been in the garage for a while. Camaros are beautiful cars. If you had this fine-looking car stashed away in your garage for a while, it may not be running as smooth as you would like. Would you want to "change it" or give it an adjustment? I am hoping you would want to give it an adjustment. If you changed it, it wouldn't be that classic 1968 Camaro anymore. What a waste. All people are beautiful in their own way and don't need to change per se; they may just need an adjustment.

Have you been picking the wrong people, or have you been searching and searching and not finding anyone? Have you spent days and nights on the internet looking for that special someone, only to find yourself emailing constantly, texting and maybe drinking too much coffee? Then, when you finally meet that special someone, being shocked to find that their face doesn't match their picture? To your horror, the web information doesn't even come close to who that person *really* is. Have you ever wondered why you read all those self-help books and why many of them tell you that you need to change in order to find the right person for you? They give you all these rules, and if you don't follow them just right, then—oh no, woe is you!—you've just blown it. After which of course you have to buy another self-help book to find out what you did wrong. The books keep telling you that you need to change. You ask yourself, "What is wrong with me?"

The truth is that there is nothing wrong with you. You are a success because what you have been doing has gotten you to where you are now. You have made it. You are a success.

The question is: Is this where you want to stay? Is what you are doing working for you, or do you want to move on to something bigger and better? I'm from Houston, and Texans are taught that bigger is better. Of course, that is not necessarily true. But try telling that to a Texan.

If what you are doing is not working for you, then you may want to think about taking a different direction. Think of yourself driving down Interstate 10 in your brand-new convertible. All you need to do is follow the highway all the way to sunny California. Oh no, there is a bunch of construction going on, and you are not able to continue on I-10. Does that mean that you are "stuck" and are not going to get to your destination—good ol' sunny California? Of course not. You have been waiting all year for this vacation. You are not going to let some construction stop you, so you take a detour or choose another direction to take you to your destination. That's how I'd like you to think of your life. You are still going for the same goal (finding a special someone), but all you are doing is taking a different road. How thrilling! What an exciting adventure you are on. Who knows what you will pass along the way.

This book is promoting you being you and finding authenticity so that you can find the same in someone else. Are you sick of playing games and going back and forth in the dating scene not knowing where you stand? Being "real" is key, and knowing what "real" means to you is important. You will learn how to appreciate being yourself, realizing there are people out there who will love you for who you are. This book will build your confidence by teaching you what to do on dates and by teaching successful secrets on how easy it is to encounter people. The goal is to promote liaisons between both men and women through meetings at local places. You will be open to meet people anywhere you go, whether you are at a grocery store, restaurant or doctor's office.

One of the bigger problems that have caused people to become more isolated in America is being stuck in social media. If you saw the movie *The Social Network* (about the founding of Facebook), then you might have thought how cool it is that more people are getting together now. But think about it. It is mostly all cyberspace, two-dimensional. It is virtual, "unreal." No one is touching, smiling or breathing on each other. We are alone, connecting! Think of what is happening to our communication skills. Our nation has lost the art of communicating and flirting because of over use of technology. *Flirting*. That's my favorite pastime. What fun people are missing! People have become addicted to technology, thinking that hitting buttons is more fun than physically seeing someone laugh at your jokes or physically having someone you like brush up against you or your arm when in a crowded room. People are usually texting instead of verbally and physically communicating because (people tell me) it is easier and less stressful on them. Therefore, people in our society are losing the ability to read and give verbal and physical cues in our three-dimensional world. Great communication takes practice. As with any activity, it takes practice to be proficient.

The majority of people I talk to who are in their 20s and 30s tell me how they "talk" to their partners all week long. When I ask if they are texting or talking, they answer, "Oh, texting." Texting has become the new talking. I remember when being verbal meant *talking*. This is causing problems in relationships because more than 50 percent of communication is exhibited by the body. This book's goal is to teach people the *Path to Genuine Connections thru Bempathy*®, a unique approach to communication and social skills, combining banter with empathy to build and maintain harmonious relationships. People want to be heard and listened to, and that can't be done through a text or email. Texting is supposed to be the least intimate of any form of communication. Then why is it so prevalent? Why do people complain that texting causes issues in their relationships, yet they keep on doing it?

There have been numerous changes throughout the years in the dating scene. When my son was 20 years old he called me up to talk about how he wanted to go on a date with an 18 year old girl. I said, "When are you going to ask her out?" He said, "Mom, that's not how it's done anymore." He explained that girls like to go out in groups of guys and girls. If the situation is one on one they feel uncomfortable and start asking questions (on the first date) such as: "Is this a date? Where is this going? What is going to happen next?" This happens because there is a lack of awareness of verbal and physical cues, along with a lack of ability to read them. People today are so into texting that when they are confronted with a "real" person they become uncomfortable. They are unable to read the cues. This is causing them to miss out on dating. This appears to be causing high anxiety and people to ask a lot of awkward questions. Therefore, kids aren't dating anymore; they are "grouping." When they are grouping they are texting each other instead of looking into the other person's eyes and talking. What is the world coming to?

"Communication" is an interesting word. People love to use different words for communication to make it sound more effective or more meaningful, such as "teamwork."

Teamwork does sound good in itself, doesn't it? Which team do you want to be on? The team of technology, of texting, emailing and game playing, or the team of smiling, touching, hugging and verbally talking. I know which team I'm on. I'm a woman, and people who know me will tell you I love to talk. Verbally that is!

Learning to be comfortable with yourself will help you to verbally communicate with others. I am not saying that meeting people online is bad, as there are cases where people end up marrying those they meet online. I am just saying that it is different, and it needs to be done with caution. I just got off the phone with a dear friend of mine who appeared to become upset with me when I spoke about how healthy it is to meet people in person rather than on the internet. She proceeded to raise her voice, saying that she was not only going to get on one app but on three apps—dating apps, that is. What do you all think of that? We are talking about dating, meeting one special person. Here I had a beautiful woman in her 30s telling me that she would rather get on three apps to meet "men" instead of going out in the real world and meeting them. I agreed with her that technology has made it easier to meet people through the internet, which does not mean healthier. Most of the single males I have spoken with prefer NOT to go online and would rather meet women in public if they had a choice. They feel that there are too many women to choose from on the internet, that it causes confusion and that it is a lot of work.

Does this remind you of you? Have you been on all those dating sites looking for that special someone only to find so many people there that you end up not knowing who to choose? When you do find that special someone and you finally go on that first date, you both "appear" to have a great time. Then why does that man or woman never answer or return your calls??? How about that guy who texted to tell you he had a great time, and then you never heard from him again. Ghosted! What happened?

Well, think of yourself as being in your favorite candy store. Yup, that's right, you can have any candy you wish. Wow, hundreds to choose from right at your fingertips! Each one is better than the next. Yum! Right? Wrong!!! With so many options it's hard to be satisfied with just one. The same thing is happening on most internet dating sites. No, I am not saying I don't recommend the sites. What I am saying is that making decisions is difficult. The more choices, the more work we have to do. We become overloaded by the number of options. We become unable to cope. Believe it or not, all these wonderful choices may also increase our regret for the ones we didn't make and leave us more disappointed with ourselves if our decisions turn out to be bad ones.

Barry Schwartz, a professor of psychology at Swarthmore College and author of the 2004 book, *The Paradox of Choice: Why More is Less*, says that one of these three things is likely to occur when people have too many decisions to make: 1) People may make poor decisions, 2) People may be more dissatisfied with their choices, or 3) People may become paralyzed and not choose at all. A 2012 Los Angeles Times article cites research that shows that "too many choices can tax the brain."

Reading this book will help you to find the perfect person for you by simply lifting your head from your phone and looking! Yes, you will learn how to attract the person who fits your puzzle. Remember, I am not dismissing the dating sites. I am just insisting there are other options, such as remembering that the "real" world is out there. You may find that it is more fun than the internet.

The great thing about this book is that it will help anyone from teenagers to seniors find and have fun with that special someone. This book is not the usual dating book intended for women. This book is for both men and women because we all are searching for the one thing: Love. Yes, men want love too. This is therefore an easy read, helping anyone to find that special someone in this fast-paced technological world we live in.

There are many books out there that tell you to "write down what you want in the other person," which is important, but what about YOU? Who are you? What are your values, your wants and your needs? Before we can find that special someone, we need to find that special someone in us.

Before you go on to the next chapter, think a bit about what made you pick up this book. Are you looking for help in specific areas of relationships? Are you looking to stop a particular pattern of picking the wrong people? Do you have some ideas about how you'd like your relationships to be different? Finding out who you are and loving who you are will attract the same type of person, which is what you want. The next chapters go into detail about how to help you meet that perfect person for you.

The great thing about this book is that you can skip around and read the chapters that apply to you. You only need to read the chapters that interest you. Feel free to skip the chapters that you believe aren't relevant. You don't need to read the entire book to benefit from it. There are no rules, only consequences. No one needs to be fixed. You are not broken.

If you are frustrated with your present situation, wondering why you can't find anyone who you're attracted to or why you're picking the wrong partners, then this book is for you. Have faith, believe that you will find that special someone, and be open to the possibilities. In my practice I see about 50 percent men and 50 percent women looking for someone to relate to. It is surprising to see that men want to find someone special too. It is not just women. What's even more surprising is that many people in their 20s and 30s find themselves talking about how hard it is to meet that special someone.

Relationships are fun. If you look up "relationship" in Webster's Dictionary it says: 1) The state of being related or interrelated, 2) A romantic or passionate attachment, and 3) A kinship. Which definition fits you? Sometimes going a different direction is a lot smoother, and with better scenery. Let's take a trip through this book and see where it may lead you.

Bempathy® Tip:

Communication *must be practiced in order to become proficient at it. An increase in* **comfortability** *with yourself promotes easier and healthier* **communication** *with others.*

CHAPTER 4

U R a Gift;
Promoting Self-Esteem

I know you want to get right down to the nitty-gritty of finding that perfect person for you. First and foremost you need to find out who you are. This chapter will encourage you to love who you are, imperfections and all, and to build self-confidence. John Legend's song that he wrote for his wife called "All of Me" says it all. For someone to fall in love with you, you need first to fall in love with yourself.

My mom had a company called U R Unique. Remember your uniqueness the first time you start to compare yourself to someone else. We are all unique, and we all have a special gift. What is yours? That is what this chapter is about—to find out what your special gift is so that it can be received and slowly—yes, I said *slowly*—unwrapped. One of the issues in this fast-paced technological world is that we want to rush everything. However, we are still human and can't always be rushed. That goes for both men and women.

People sometimes feel bored with themselves or become stuck finding the same type of people or doing the same type of things. Being stuck creates stress, stress creates unhappiness, unhappiness creates discouragement, discouragement creates frustration, and frustration creates being stuck. There you have it. People then start to look for excitement, possibly a dramatic relationship to make them feel alive. Or they may jump from job to job. How do you put excitement in your life? Is the excitement working for you? What motivates you? What is your dream?

I remember a short adage from when I was younger that said, "Keep on Trucking." In other words, keep on moving after you stumble. How many people do you know who have failed at something, or better yet failed at a lot of things? Did you know that the more you fail the more successful you are? How many babies do you know who popped out of their mom, put on some sneakers and ran a race? If you know of any, give them to me. I could make a mint.

What really happens is that after babies are born they *progressively* sit up, crawl and then stand while holding onto things. When babies do start to walk they stumble and fall just like we do in life. When babies fall, what do they do? Do they just stay on the ground and cry and never get up again? They may feel like it, but they not only get up, they get up and do an even better job at it. By the time they are six or seven they may even be proficient at running. It may take many failures to become a success. We need to fail before we can succeed.

> *They say that time changes things, but you actually have to*
> *change them yourself.*
> Andy Warhol

The same happens in life. We stumble and fall/fail at relationships. Some of us move on and learn; others get stuck and need a push. This book is to help give you a push. The importance of this chapter is to help you attract the person that fits your puzzle. Have you ever put a puzzle together and tried to fit a piece into it that just didn't quite fit? What happened? Maybe it went in (begrudgingly) with some extra space around it or no space at all, or maybe it just fell out. When you find that perfect piece, it just seems to slide on in. That is what you are looking for. That perfect piece that fits you perfectly.

- Believe in yourself
- Have faith in yourself, life and others

Baggage

Sometimes we are weighed down by the past. We hold onto baggage and bring it into another relationship. Think of it as that piece from the puzzle that you are just trying to shove in. When this happens in a relationship, you may feel that there is too much space or too little space, or the person and you keep sliding back and forth. Some people think that they or the other person is playing games. More likely "baggage" is preventing them from getting too close. Think of baggage as 1) weighing you down and 2) a barrier preventing you from getting too close to the other person involved. I have a saying about baggage:

"When we bring the past to the present it becomes our future."

Think about it. When we continue to talk about bad past relationships, when we continue to talk about divorce, when we continue to blame someone in the past for where we are at this moment, it keeps us stuck there. It keeps us stuck in the past.

You want to move on and yet be aware of the past. The past is important because it makes you who you are today—a wonderful human being looking for someone with whom to share all this wonder. Remember that the past helps our intuition, but it can also hinder relationships. It can be a double-edged sword. If we have anger toward a past relationship, remember that it is in the *past,* and don't bring it into your present relationship. Just increasing your awareness of how the past affects you will help you to move on to your next great adventure.

For example, just because you have a history of burning relationships in which the flame rapidly goes out doesn't mean that the same will happen in your next relationship. Learn from the past in a *positive* way. Like a baby walking. A baby stumbles and falls, gets up and takes another step, which may be even steadier. Pretty soon he is off to the races.

Think of baggage as barriers, walls that prevent you from moving on. Let's remember President Reagan's speech in Berlin and "tear down those walls." Just like the Berlin Wall, all walls keep things in and keep things out. By breaking down those walls you are making the world your oyster. You will be free to pick and choose whatever comes your way instead of sabotaging or pushing people away. You will have more options.

Just because the past didn't turn out like you wanted it to, doesn't mean your future can't be better than you ever imagined.
Anonymous

Check the obstacles below that may be preventing you from moving on to your prime goal of companionship:

- guilt
- anger
- substance abuse
- wearing a mask
- worry
- fear
- resentment
- inability to let go
- pride
- not forgiving
- hurt
- unaccepting
- pretending
- indecisive

- workaholic
- blame
- avoidance
- lying to self
- confusion
- being stuck
- making excuses
- grief
- rigidity
- intellectualizing
- shame
- avoidance
- _____
- _____
- _____
- _____
- _____
- _____

Turn your baggage into motivators. Turning your baggage and imperfections into motivators will help increase your self-esteem. Strong self-esteem makes people feel powerful. Power helps to exude confidence. Confidence is sexy. Sexy attracts a mate. Wow! Sounds good to me. How about you?

Take for example, "fear." Instead of letting fear block you from being emotionally intimate or preventing you from even pursuing a relationship, have fear motivate you. Have it motivate you to go out and make yourself the best you can be. It's like going on a scary ride at the carnival. You may fear it, but you can still take that ride and feel exhilarated at the end.

Have you ever met someone who rushes into a relationship, gets sexually intimate and then pulls away? Notice I said "sexually" intimate. Just because you are being sexual doesn't mean you are close. Yes, you are intimate, but it may be just on the sexual side. Sometimes that can get in the way of really getting to know someone. Your physical chemistry even changes when you have sex. That is why it feels so good, but it may prevent you from seeing your situation clearly.

Everyone asks me how long they need to wait to have sex when dating. Remember, I keep saying that this isn't a game, and I mean it. Think of people in general. Think of yourself for a moment. When you work really hard to get something—a house, a car or finishing school—how do you feel once you have accomplished it? Great, right? Well, think of a relationship in the same way. If it is too easy, we as humans don't appreciate it as much as if we had worked hard at it. There is no set time or day to have sex. The timing depends on you. If in your past history you were having sex with your significant other after the third date and it wasn't working, then slow it down by half. It needs to feel right for both parties. It is important for both parties to feel safe.

There are no rules on how long to wait to be physically intimate. The issue about having sex too early is that after sexual intercourse there is a hormone released in the body for both men and women that causes them to feel attached even if they don't know each other's names. For men the hormone is called *vasopressin* and for women it is called *oxytocin*. The problem is that this is chemical, not mental. Love takes time. Think about eating your favorite food. Is it better to savor every bite or just to demolish it? The same goes for a relationship that is just beginning. Take it slow and easy. This time will never be here again. Savor every minute of your new beginning together by getting to know who that person really is.

A great saying to remember is: "True Love Takes Time."

Ask yourself, "Is this a person who I want for the long term?" If the answer is yes, then you have a lifetime to experience the sexual act. You have a lifetime to be together.

According to a study that appeared in the "Journal of Family Psychology," couples who delayed sexual activities appear to have more stable and happier marriages. Researchers have noted that there is a definite correlation between waiting to become sexually involved and having better relationship satisfaction, stability, communication and sexual quality in marriage.

Think of yourself as a gift that needs to be slowly unwrapped to be appreciated and savored. In this chapter you will slowly unwrap your special gift and then be able to fully share it with whomever you choose. It will be your choice. You are in control. Doesn't it feel good just saying, "I am in control"?

Write this down on paper and say it every day: "I am in control."

Journal

Writing in a journal may help you to get to know what your baggage is. When I was younger, journaling got a bad rap. We used to call them "diaries." My brothers called them "diarrheas." Journals are a good source for seeing patterns that may be keeping you from getting the sweetheart that you want. They also will help you to find out what your gift or talent may be. Sometimes, even reading your journal out loud and recording it, then playing it back to actually hear it, helps you make even better sense of things.

I tell people to think about when they were younger. What gave them pleasure? What did they always dream of doing?

If you are a person that jumps from job to job, or relationship to relationship, remember that you are the common denominator. You have control over you; therefore, you have control over how your movie plays out. You are the hero or heroine of your own screenplay. Let's begin to write an awesome one by starting with that journal. You can title it, "I'm in control."

You are on your way to overcoming fear of commitment by learning to commit to yourself and realizing that you not only have a gift, you are one.

Most of us have some baggage. It is important to realize that. When we start feeling fear, resentment, anger or sadness, think about where those feelings are coming from. What are the triggers? Talk it over with a nonjudgmental friend, counselor or life coach before you jump to a poor conclusion and push your person away or sabotage what you have or what you want.

Holding on to anger is like holding on to a hot coal with the intent of throwing it at someone else; you are the one who gets burned.

Buddha

Let's start to get to know ourselves.

- What do you love most about yourself?
- Who are you?

Did you ever see the movie "Anger Management" with Jack Nicholson and Adam Sandler? There is a great scene in which Sandler is in group therapy and Nicholson asks him, "Tell us about yourself." It was funny because Sandler kept telling the group about himself but it wasn't what they wanted to hear. If you ever get a chance, watch it. It may help you with this part of the book.

First Sandler tells them what he does as a professional. Then Nicholson says he doesn't want him to tell them what he does for a living. Then Sandler talks about his hobbies. Nicholson again responds by saying they don't want to know about his hobbies. Nicholson again asks him to tell him about himself. Sandler ends with talking about how he is a nice guy and easy going. Nicholson then says, "Don't tell us your personality. We want to know who you are."

So who are you? That movie clip, though funny, probably made you think. This portion of the book is about getting to know what your gift or talent is. This is more than knowing your hobbies, your profession or your personality—though that is all part of who you are. Your gift or talent is something that you do that is noteworthy. For example, President Obama is known for his speaking, and President Reagan was known for his humor. Reagan even made a joke when he was shot. Knowing your gift will help you attract that special someone. Think of yourself as a total package.

When you meet someone new who asks, "Tell me about yourself,"

- Do you become speechless?
- Do you tell them what your gift is?

A talent is something you can do easily. We all have one. Think about things you enjoy. Think of something you felt good about doing. People usually enjoy doing things that come easily to them. Some examples of talents (gifts) are:

- music
- athletic ability
- language
- leadership
- public speaking

- organizing
- listening
- mechanical
- sense of humor
- relating to animals

What are talents/gifts?

Doing the below exercises are not only going to increase your confidence, they will also affect your body language. Think about it. When you feel good about yourself, how do you walk? Sure, your posture becomes erect, your stance may appear more relaxed, your eye contact more direct, and your tone and volume in your voice may change. You may even smile more. All this makes you more appealing to people, especially people to whom you may be attracted.

Want to build self-assurance? Then make a list of your talents. Some examples are listed above.

_____

_____

_____

_____

_____

_____

Knowing what you are good at and doing more of it will help to build self-confidence.

Now practice bringing more of these talents into your life to increase your self-esteem. The more you use your talents, the more poise you bring to yourself and the easier it is to believe that someone special is going to fall for you.

There are groups called *meet ups* in which people engage with other people while applying their talents. These groups are also known as a type of support group.

Healthy support groups

What is a support group?

I usually use the analogy of a support bra. Yes, even men are good at answering this question. You'd be surprised. The question is:

What does a support bra do for you?

- It lifts you up.
- It holds you together.
- It keeps you safe.
- It keeps you stable.
- It makes you feel confident.
- It makes you feel comfortable.
- It makes you feel safe.

- It makes you look great (if not, I hope you get a new support bra).
- It helps to point you in the right direction.

A support group does the same minus the breasts. What I mean is, people in a support group will do for you the same thing that a support bra does for a woman's chest. If you are not feeling comfortable, if people don't make you feel good, if you don't feel safe, then you need to be hanging around different people that do what a support bra does. It's important to be with people who support you, lift you up and help hold you together. So the next time you are with people, think of a support bra. Be with the types of people who help build your self-esteem and confidence. They will lift you up like a support bra rather than drag you down like extra baggage.

The point of this chapter is to feel good about who you are. Accept your imperfections and emphasize your gifts. Accentuate the positive and eliminate the negative. Focus on your positive attributes and realize that no one is perfect. John Legend's song "All of Me" says it all: "Love . . . all your perfect imperfections." The game below is something that I share with my clients so that they are able to realize that all in life is fleeting.

The temporary game

If and when you talk about your imperfections (which I am sure are few) use the *Temporary Game*. This is how it works: You say a negative comment about yourself, and then you add the word "temporarily." It works great. For example: I am not good in relationships "temporarily" *(for right now/at this time)*. This means that for the time being you may feel and believe this to be true; however, it is NOT lasting. Just like everything in this world, it is temporary. Doing this will help you to put up with the sad times and appreciate the happy times. It will help to put things in perspective.

You don't have to think positive or use the temporary game. Actually there are no "have to's" in this world of ours. Friends have argued with me about this, stating we have to do a lot of "stuff" in this world to get what we want. Let me explain how this principle works:

The "no have to's" principle

No have to's

Just consequences

So I want to

There are no "have to's" in this world except to be born and to die. You don't have to work, to eat, to exercise or sleep. What this theory is saying is that there are no "have to's." There are only consequences that lead to "want to's." Think about it. If you don't go to work, there are consequences to your actions. Consequences can be either positive or negative, and they will help guide you to a "want to."

Consequences are what we believe them to be. This is where our values come into play. A person to whom I told this theory said, "Jill I love the "no have to's" principle. I said, "What do you mean?" She answered, "Well, Friday I didn't feel like going to work. I was not feeling the best, and I said to myself, 'Jill said I don't have to go to work today.' Then I thought, if I don't go to work today, some of my peers may be resentful, I won't get paid, I might get in trouble and I might lose my job. So then I said, 'mmm, I want to go to work,' and I ended up having an awesome day." Remember, this is just a theory that seems to work for my clients and myself. Have fun with this.

So let me put this to the men out there: You don't have to ask a woman out. If you don't, you have a 100 percent chance of failure. If you choose to ask her out, you have a 50/50 chance of success. She will most likely either say yes or no. People either do it or they don't. They don't just try candy; they eat it. You tell me which is better for you. Do you want to be a spectator or a participant in your search for a partner?

In effect, this is how the "no have to's" principle works. It has helped people reduce their anxiety level and make their life more enjoyable. That is what we may be looking for—a wonderful journey to happiness and success. We want to do things because we choose to, not because we have to.

Therefore, when you read this book please remember that there are no "have to's." Instead, look at the consequences and ask yourself if that is how you want to live. You can use some of the information you read if you "want to." Some of the information you can put in file 13. It is your choice. Use what works for you. Remember, we are all unique.

Now that you realize that you have a special gift, I want you to think of your entire being as "the total package." Finding that special person within yourself will help you attract someone else who is also the "total package." Think of yourself as a gift that wants to be admired and appreciated. You are a gift, slowly floating down a river, easily gliding over and around the rocks. When you reach your destination you will be slowly unwrapped and found out to be the exceptional prize that you are. You are someone authentic, independent and with wonderful self-confidence, getting ready to share your awesomeness with someone else.

Notice that I said, "Glide over the rocks." Some people like to hold onto the rocks to feel safe because they don't know what is downriver. These people might feel stuck in their present situation. The unknown can be scary. It can also be exciting. Mystery can be stimulating and intriguing. Mystery is what is missing in this technological world of ours. Everything is put "out there" in virtual reality. Or is it?

When doing a seminar, a man from the audience told me how he had met this beautiful girl at a concert and gotten her number. Then he proceeded to tell me that he looked her up on social networking sites and that she didn't look as pretty as he remembered. He also commented that he didn't like what she had to say on her social media platforms. You got it. He didn't call her because of

Facebook, TikTok, etc. And she missed out on having a date from an attractive man. In the "old days," a man met you, liked you, got your number and called. There are many stories, including one from Dr. Sherry Turkle, about people misrepresenting themselves. One such (very funny) story she told was about an elderly man from a nursing home pretending to be a "sexy hot babe in Memphis" because he was bored. The person on the other end didn't think it was so funny. So let's take a journey down this river and not hold onto those rocks. Let's flow down the river, letting go of baggage, fears and technology. Okay, let's still use technology but with a little caution. In other words, let's be in control of how we use it and realize that not all is real in the virtual world.

> *You cannot step twice into the same river, for other*
> *waters are continually flowing in.*
> Heraclitus, ca 500 BCE

A "catfish" is someone who pretends on the internet to be someone he or she is not, "just for fun." There's even a TV show now called "Catfish." Scary! Does that mean it is a good thing to pretend to be who you are not? This is something to think about if you believe in the law of attraction. The law of attraction states that we attract who we are.

Catfishing and other things that are happening on the internet should make us take note and be leery of who is on the other end of a "two-dimensional" device. I suggest using communication platforms like Zoom or Face Time when you talk to people on the internet. Make sure that you talk to people on the phone as soon as possible, and don't let them know where you live until you physically meet. This way you at least know what gender they really are and a little bit about their personality. Remember that, depending on which psychologist you talk to, 50 to 60 percent of communication is nonverbal. This means that body language is a *huge* part of communication. Body language is definitely missing in a "two-dimensional" world. This goes along with what I have been talking about before, which is, "slow it down." If you are looking for a lifetime partner, what is the rush? You will have a lifetime to share with that person.

People seem to be afraid or uncomfortable being themselves. I'm here to tell you that you are special and have a unique gift to share. The important thing to realize is that there is no perfect person in this world. Wow! That sure made me feel better. How about you? Studies show that we are more comfortable with people who we believe are not perfect. That being said, what makes people want someone who is "perfect?" That is both unrealistic and dissatisfying. Think about it. We ourselves are wonderful beings, but we are far from perfect. So, how could we find someone who is? It would take a lifetime. In fact, it would take more than a lifetime because it is not going to happen. That is a positive thing. If you meet someone who has about 80 percent of what you want, then that someone is possibly the perfect person for you. Now, it needs to be the 80 percent that you can live with, and the 20 percent needs to be what you can put up with or live without. Remembering that we are not perfect takes a load off. It is a known fact that perfectionism increases anxiety. So there you go. You have just taken a load off and made it easier to find that special someone.

Forgiveness is the fragrance that the violet
sheds on the heel that has crushed it.
Mark Twain

Wants, needs and values help to define who you are. What are your wants, your needs and your values? This is something that is essential for you to know. Have you heard of the law of attraction? Think about your friends. Are they similar to you? Do they have similar values and beliefs? Probably so. We usually attract who we are. What that means is that if you are going through a divorce, putting you in flux, you may meet a person in a similar situation. He or she may be freshly divorced, never married, having problems at work, etc. That is the reason it is so important for you to be whole— so that you will attract a matching counterpart.

One of the first things that I suggest is to write down your wants in life. They need to be written in such a way that you are not giving mixed messages. For example, if you say, "I want less stress," then your brain is going to hear "stress." It is as though you are really asking to have more stress in your life. It would be better to say and think, "I want peacefulness." Mixed messages will prevent you from getting what you really want. If you were in a relationship and you crossed your arms, yelling in a gruff tone, "I love you, give me a hug," do you think you're going to get some loving? I doubt it. This is what happens when we say we want a certain type of person but seem to get the opposite, the bad guy or the unemotional woman. It's because of how we write or think of our wants. We may be giving mixed signals. One day a man said to me that he loves it when a woman calls him, but after being challenged he changed his mind saying, "You are right, I enjoy the chase."

Really listen to what people say to you and watch their entire being. Here this man would tell women to call him because he thought that is what he really wanted, but it wasn't. Then he wondered why he was attracting the wrong women for him. This is an example of the importance of really knowing what you want.

Ask yourself, "Do I want a pick up or to meet someone special? Do I want an appetizer or a whole meal? Do I want a night or a life changing event?" Knowing what you want will help you start attracting it.

Write down at least ten wants. Be specific, and remember to be positive. If you are having trouble doing this, then think about what you don't want. Draw a line down the middle of your paper. On the left side write down everything you don't want. For some reason this is easier for most people. Then on the right side of the paper write the exact opposite of what you wrote on the left side of the paper. Of course tear up the "don't want" list. You want to attract in your life what you "want."

I want:

_____

_____

_____

_____

_____

_____

Now let's get to know ourselves even better by asking ourselves what our values are.

What do values tell you about a person? Believe it or not, knowing your values gives us direction and identity. Values are our beliefs about what is right for us. Values are most likely developed in the first ten to twelve years of life. What we value can change throughout life.

What do you value? Below are some examples of values. Take this time and check your own values:

- love
- work
- health
- money
- time
- achievement
- leisure
- power

- relationships
- spiritual
- pleasure
- education
- honesty
- security
- prestige
- helping others
- arts

List more if need be:

_____

_____

_____

_____

_____

_____

Prioritize your values by putting down what you value most as number one. Ask yourself, "Am I satisfying my values in my life? Is my behavior matching my values?" For example, if you value family, is your behavior in agreement with that value—that family is very important to you? If not, what would it take to fulfill your values? What type of behavior do you need to exhibit to match your values?

Values affect the way you deal with your family, your friends and your entire life. They are sometimes difficult to live by, which can cause conflict, anxiety and affect your self-esteem. The more our behavior matches our values the better we feel about ourselves. Ask yourself, "Does my behavior match my values?" If not, this is something for you to think about working on. Remember that people aren't perfect and that there are no "have to's." This is when you think about the consequences of not following through with your values. The same can be said for dating. Yes, the more the person we are with reflects our values, the more compatible we are with that person. All your values do not need to match. But let's just say that the more your values match the other person's, the less complicated the relationship may be. This is the reason it is important to know *your* wants and *your* values. Knowing and being aware of what you value will help you attract the same in another person.

This chapter is going to help you build your self-esteem to the point where you will be exuding so much self-confidence that it will overflow to others. Think of yourself as a milk carton. If you keep pouring the milk out, what happens? The carton becomes empty. Have you ever felt that way? Empty? What if you fill the milk carton up and continue to fill it until it overflows? That is what happens when you are filled with self-assurance. Did you know that confidence is extremely sexy? We are not talking about our outer appearance; we are talking about our inner self. Being sexy sells itself.

You see it in charismatic people like Oprah, Duchess Kate, George Clooney, President Reagan, President Clinton and Beyoncé. You too can have this charisma by working on the exercises in this chapter. These exercises will help increase your awareness of who you are and what you want in another person. The more you know who you are and start fulfilling your wants, the more your self-esteem will run over and shine for others to see and gravitate toward.

Remember, likes attract like. Keep a focus on what and who you want to attract.

Bempathy Tip:

*Much of **communication** is behavioral. Be aware of what your behavior is saying to others and vice versa.*

CHAPTER 5

Going Fishing

Fishing. Is that what you sometimes feel you are doing when you are on dating apps, in a bar, or at a party weeding out all those sharks? Going fishing can be a wonderful sport—calming, relaxing, and sometimes worth the wait. True fishermen are patient and endure the storms and rocky waters to catch a long waited for special fish.

When you fish for salmon, you use different bait/outfits/equipment etc. than when you fish for sharks or trout. The same is true when meeting different kinds of people. Dating is like fishing. If you know what you want, then you use a certain bait to get it. This may sound like a game, but it is not. It is the way of life. In the animal world the male usually is the one that attracts the mate. He is colorful and maybe does a dance or two. He needs to be in the right location. Sometimes none of it works, and he needs to find another female to woo. So it goes in the human world as well. The only difference is that today we are going to compare dating to fishing so that you will know exactly how to enhance all your wonderful attributes. Remember there are no "have to's" and no rules you *must* follow, just consequences to your actions. In this book there are recommendations that will help make you feel more confident and maybe spice up your first meeting.

You need a KAAAP (cap) for fishing:

1. Know what to expect (expectations)
2. A strong line with a good hook (to hook them in)
3. An inviting fishing spot
4. Appropriate bait, possibly a lure (depending upon what you are looking for)
5. Patience is a virtue

#1. *Let's start with "expectations."* Great expectations can get us into trouble. Expectations can lead us to disappointments, especially when they involve "have to's." He or she *has to* be a certain way or I won't go out with them. This closes the doors to what could be a great catch of the day. Open yourself up to what life has to offer. This increases opportunities. You might be surprised by what you reel in. Keep your eyes open for fascinating possibilities.

Every time you leave your home, have the mind-set that you are going for an interview for a date with someone special, or, as stated in this chapter, that you are going fishing. In other words, be *prepared*. You never know where that "big fish" is going to show up. It might be in deep or shallow waters, a small or a large pool, or just right in your front yard. This is the way to think—in terms of opportunities.

What do you expect in a partner? We tend to choose partners who:

- Help us meet our present needs
- Fulfill our expectations
- Work through our issues
- Grow with us

What's the difference between pickups and meeting people?

A. The start may be the same, the ending is different

B. Appetizer versus a meal

C. Night or a week versus a life changing event

Expectation; what is yours?

Your expectations may not be working for you. Let me explain. Yes, it is good to have high values or wants. However our values and wants may affect our expectations. When people's behaviors don't match their values, complications may evolve. Our values are what we believe to be right for us, not for someone else. This comes up in politics and religion all the time. Raising kids is just one of the topics that is affected by our values. That is a good reason not to bring up values on a first date. It could bring on complications even before you both really get to know each others' personalities. The first meeting basically is to see if your personalities match and if you like each other.

Realizing that our values and wants may be good for us doesn't mean that we all have to have the same values. Remember the "no have to's" principle? It means, among other things, that similar values make for a less complicated meet up. If you value family, and the other person values family, then your personal rules will be similar. It is up to us to know what we can live with and what we can live without. Compromise does not mean "settling." It means that you have some values and wants that you cannot live without and others that are not as important.

An example: You may value family as a number one priority, and your partner may value career/achievements as a number one priority. What problems do you think might occur? Have you ever met someone who worked all the time? When you invited that person to a family function they may have been caught at work and ended up attending the family function late. You couldn't understand why they didn't feel the same as you about the importance of that family function. You may have felt hurt, mad, frustrated and embarrassed that they were late to something so important to you. But what happened was that they were into their work and enjoying what they were doing and only going to the function to please you. Family didn't have the same importance for them that it has for you. Therefore, the person was late. Some people may have missed the function altogether. Do you see what I am getting at? No one is playing games with you; it's just that the other person's values may be slightly different from yours.

If this is a value that you can't live without, then this would be a red flag. This is something to be aware of. If there is hope, it's because values can change. However, the problem is that we only have control over ourselves. People change only if they want to. Please don't go into a relationship hoping to change the other person. That is an expectation that may cause great disappointment.

> *The weak can never forgive, forgiveness*
> *is the attribute of the strong.*
> Mahatma Gandhi

The fourth chapter helped you to understand the important role your values play in self-esteem and attracting a mate. The following will help you to know if that sexy person sitting across from you has similar values to yours. How do you know if your values match? Good question. Behavior such as pointed out in the above paragraph will tell you how well your values match and if the match is something you can live with. Remember, no one is perfect, including you. When your values get in the way of who is right or wrong, it may be a good time to ask yourself if you would rather be *right* or *happy*.

Remember that like attracts like. I am not talking about personality. Different personalities can be great together. I am talking about having things in common—likes, wants, values, morals, beliefs, etc. Ask yourself, "Does this person have most of my wants, likes, morals and values?"

Silence is golden when it comes to fishing. There is so much you can learn from observation alone. When fishing for a partner and wanting to know if they match your wants, remember to "stop, look and listen." This gets you to:

- Take a moment to observe
- Increase your awareness of their behavior
- Listen to who they are
- See red flags
- Listen to red flags (people mean what they say when they say it)
- Go with caution
- Listen to their "shoulds" in conversation (they are their rules and values)
- Decide how many red flags are too many
- Understand that too many red flags could mean you need to go to another fishing spot

Identify the relationship you are seeking

Are you looking for a long-term relationship, a short-term relationship, marriage, etc.? Are you looking for an appetizer or a full course meal? In other words, are you looking for the whole enchilada? If you expect to meet that specific companion, then the first thing to do is to write a list of what you want in a partner. Notice I say "partner" because that means both men and women. Experts will tell you to write down what you want in your partner. I tell my clients to do the following:

- Draw a straight line down the middle of a page
- On the left side write down all the traits of past partners that you could NOT live with
- On the right side write down the opposite traits
- Then rip up the negative side and keep the positive side
- If you have never had a relationship, then write down traits you want in a mate
- On the positive side continue to add or take away traits from the list until you meet your partner
- Make sure "emotionally available" and "respectful" are at the top of the list. For some reason people forget to put these down.

Note: It is very important to tear up the left side of the page because you *do not* want to attract the negative traits.

A person who attended one of my lectures complained how the list she made wasn't working. She had made a list of traits that she wanted in a man and kept getting men that weren't into her or that she had to chase. She said that she had given up and didn't want to do this anymore. I looked at her list and said that she was attracting everything she had put on that particular list. She was a success, though not a success in finding what she wanted in the first place. Then I asked her to do the above exercise. What she found was that the new list attracted the men who gave her pleasure instead of frustration. It is important to know what we are attracting. We do the picking, not the other way around. We might not have control over whom we are attracted to; but we are in control over whom we choose. We are in control of our lives, not the other person. So go for it.

When you write your list you can add and delete traits as you go through the dating process. "Emotionally available" is recommended to be number one. If someone is not emotionally available, then it is futile to go further unless you are not looking for a long-term relationship. Here is an example of my list that helped me to meet my husband. Have fun making your own.

- Emotionally available
- Respectful
- Good chemistry
- Good sense of humor
- Zero to two kids
- Married no more than once
- Emotionally stable
- Laid back with a lot of energy
- Considerate of my needs (empathetic)
- Caring
- Well established/monetarily stable
- Ambitious
- Giving
- Willing to learn new fun things to do together

- Open to seeking therapy

- Dependable

- Trusting and confidential

- Nonjudgmental

- Affectionate (loves sex)

- Supportive

- Positive

- Able to compromise

Dreamboat poster

The dreamboat poster is something to have fun with. There are no "have to's." You may not want to put into pictures what you want or are looking for. You may want to leave it to your imagination, similar to when you read a book and imagine the hero to look a certain way. Then you see the movie, and it may be ruined for you because the actor picked to play the hero does not match who you envisioned. Therefore, if you decide to make your dreamboat poster, make the heroes all look different. Cut out different looks of what your dreamboat may be. This will keep your options more open to different looks and presentations. Making the dreamboat poster will be fun and will help you to focus on the positives you are looking for.

Remember when you were younger and you met your "true love" or your first love? What did you do all day? You probably thought of how wonderful they were, drew hearts with both of your names on it, and fantasized what you would be doing with them. You may have basically thought about them all day long. As you got older it may have gotten more difficult to fantasize about what type of person you want. Sometimes it is hard to see what kind of person you want, especially if you have not had great role models in your life. The purpose of the dreamboat poster is for you to actually *see* a person exhibiting traits that you wish them to have—through pictures and not just words! It may help you to envision what and how you want them to be. Take the traits that you just wrote down and put the "words" on a cork board. Beside the words put a picture of a person who matches the traits that you want. For example, if one of the traits is "emotionally available," put a picture next to that trait of someone holding hands with someone else, both hands with wedding rings on their ring fingers. Or next to the trait of 'healthy" put a picture of someone exercising and eating well. This will help you do the next step, which will be envisioning meeting this person. When cutting out your pictures, remember that the person doesn't have to look the same in each picture. That way you will be open to more than one type of look.

Screenplay

Write a script of your fantasy person, the person of your dreams, the person that you have always wanted to be a part of your life. This is your play, so have fun with it. It is important to realize in your fantasy that no one is perfect, not even you. So don't think "Cinderella Story." I hope I didn't burst your bubble. Just because the other person won't be perfect doesn't mean your fantasy won't be fantastic. Think about who the perfect person is for you. Now that you have your dreamboat poster, it may help you to picture that person. Write in detail how the first meeting takes place and what you will be doing when you meet. Write how the relationship progresses and how you want it to progress.

Visualize

How many fishermen do you know who will tell you how big their fish will be before they go out and catch them? They sit there on their boat and fantasize about their soon to be catch. Fishermen are passionate about their vision. Well, that is what you need to be.

Take five minutes and visualize the person that you just wrote about above. Imagine how your meeting is going to go down. In other words, imagine what your first date will look like. Visualize your person approaching you or you approaching them. Imagine how it flows and how the conversation just flies by. Imagine yourself being assertive and self-confident. Visualize yourself dealing effectively with the person of your dreams. In your imagery, be as much your natural self as you can be. Imagine the dialogue and how you are reacting. If you notice yourself feeling anxious at any time during your visualization, calm yourself by taking six deep breaths. When you are feeling calm, continue to visualize. This needs to be something enjoyable.

First dates are to get to know if there is an attraction, NOT to know if you are going to spend the rest of your life together. Remember, you are a Ferrari going 60 instead of 200 mph. What's the rush? In your visualization, think of this:

- KEEP IT LIGHT AND BREEZY
- HAVE FUN

Fear is a good thing. It is a motivator. Think of the excitement of doing something fearful such as going on a roller coaster, bungee jumping or doing something for the first time. Feel that feeling and go with it. On the first meeting go with:

Soft talk versus deep discussions.

1) Less is more (leave some mystery; think of cliff hangers)
2) Being aware of nervous habits (touching, fidgeting, interrogation, twitching)

An example of "soft talk" would be talking about family, fun events, travel, work, funny mishaps in sports, television shows, movies, sports announcers and leisure activities. Everyone has some nervous habit that may pop up on a first date. Having a table comes in handy both to hide your fidgety hands and to use a technique that will help you to stop and think instead of ramble.

This technique is called "Thought Stoppage." It works great to increase awareness of what you are doing. This is how it works. Put a rubber band on your wrist. That in itself will remind you to relax and listen. If you feel yourself starting to be an FBI agent and beginning to interrogate, snap your rubber band to remind yourself to stop what you are doing and change direction, or just slow down. What's the rush? If you start thinking negative thoughts during the date, snap that rubber band to change the direction of your thinking.

Think "Short and Sweet" for the first date. Mystery. Leave them wanting more or just leave without feeling that you wasted your time. A couple of hours is fine.

#2. The second element you need in getting that fish is a strong line with a sturdy hook so that once you make the catch the fish stays on the line. Remember, this is not a game. This is you being real. It is good to practice talking about yourself and to have an "elevator pitch," just as business people do. Aren't you selling yourself? In dating, as in fishing, if your line isn't strong, how do you expect to reel in the big fish? The previous chapter helped you to define yourself by knowing your wants and values. Remember, it is important that you have similar values and common interests with the other person. This knowledge will make your line stronger.

You have heard the saying, "Fake it till you make it." Well, I say, "Believe it till you receive it." We are all unique. The more you say it the more you believe it.

Elevator pitch for meeting people

Want to "break the ice?" Use an elevator pitch.

This pitch is slightly different from a business line because this pitch is both to sell yourself and draw the person into you. It needs to be short and sweet and catchy. Your pitch could be about your values/interests and wants. The purpose of this statement is to reel the person into a conversation. Pitches on a date are usually prefaced with a compliment to capture the person's attention. Then the pitch is thrown.

When you compliment the person of interest, be sure to compliment their uniqueness. For example, instead of complimenting their hair color, compliment the way they had it cut or styled. That way you are complimenting their taste, which may lead to more conversation. A suggestion for men: compliment a woman's attire, not her "derrière" or legs.

A friend once told me a story about using an opening line to get people to partner up with him to play golf. It went something like this: "Are you independently wealthy, or do you have to work for a living?" He began this way to get people to chuckle, making them feel comfortable to partner up with him in golf. The same goes for partnering up in life. The more you say your pitch, the more comfortable you will become with it, and the more comfortable other people will be when they are around you.

Using the "no have to's" principle may help motivate you to throw out your pitch. An acquaintance talked about being in the lunch room every day and not talking to anyone. When asked what he was thinking, he said, "It takes too much energy to talk to someone." When he used the "no have to's" principle, he realized that if he talked, the consequences would be that:

- He might meet someone
- He may have a better day
- He would feel better about himself

After adjusting his thinking, he said, "I want to talk to the people in the lunch room." In other words, he wanted to meet someone, to have a better day and to feel better about himself. This is another example of how the "no have to's" principle may help motivate you to get what you want.

People ask me, "Where can I find that special someone?" There are books telling people about places to go meet people. What I tell people is that every day that you leave your home you should think of it as going on an interview for a date. In other words, you can meet your person *anywhere*. The options are endless. What is great and exciting is that you don't know when it will happen.

Knowing your "great pitch" and being comfortable with it will make you emotionally comfortable, which will make you more approachable. People like people who are comfortable in their own skin.

Feel free to go online and look at business elevator pitches to see the format. Then ask yourself what you are interested in. What are you passionate about? Remember, passion is passion. It is contagious and flows onto others nearby. You've always heard that if you are passionate in what you do for work, then you will be prosperous. Similarly, if you are passionate about your interests, they will draw in the other person. Now, I am not talking about pushing your ideas onto someone. I am talking about expressing your passion and then *listening* to what the other person has to say in response. Let it flow.

The purpose of having an elevator pitch is to make you feel comfortable and at the same time draw the other person in by:

- Catching them off guard
- Reeling them in with wit
- Putting you in control of the situation
- Making both parties comfortable

Below are examples of a down to earth pitch:

1. When you see that person who's caught your attention, possibly at a golf club, wave at them to come over. After they have come over, say something like, "Do I know you from somewhere? I go to a lot of golfing events."

2. If you see someone in whom you are interested, do the "Hanky Drop"—a card or business card on which you write down your number—then say, "If you want to do lunch, give me a call. Italian is my favorite."

3. If you see a cutie in a conference room all by their lonesome self, say, "Hi. How is it having the entire conference room to yourself? I myself like doing work in this room."

4. If someone is wearing red, you could say, "Wow, red is my favorite color. My car is even that color. What about yours?"

Now you can make your own elevator pitch, causing your line to be stronger and more attractive to hook the person in. Practice makes perfect. An elevator pitch will get you comfortable with an opening line about yourself, and the conversation will have a better chance to flow.

_____

_____

_____

_____

Interrogation versus banter

When you find your fishing spot you want a steady current to prevent the water from becoming stagnant. The same goes for your conversation. If the conversation at your first meeting doesn't flow, it may become sluggish. It is important to keep the current going to keep the conversation from dying, just like at your fishing spot.

First and foremost, we are into attracting, not repelling. I will be the first to tell you that interrogating a person is a guaranteed fast way to get them to jump ship. No one wants to feel as though a lawyer is cross-examining them. So, when you go on your first date think of it as "going fishing for the night." Be cool, calm and collected. Remind yourself that there are plenty more fish where this one came from and think of this as just practice. That will take off some of the pressure. There is not just one person out there for you. People are all unique, like you, and waiting to be caught.

First meetings can be nerve racking for both parties. On the other side of the table, the person's nerves could be causing them to interrogate you because they don't know what else to do. Help them by deflecting the questions when interrogated. Think "politician." Think Presidents Reagan, Clinton or Obama. Google some of these famous politicians' debates to get some idea of how to respond without acting as though you were being attacked. Politicians are great at moving the question back to the other person by saying, with enthusiasm, "Great question. What do you think about that?" Or, "What an interesting thought. How does that relate to you?" These are just examples of how to react to questions that do not need to be answered on a first date.

A first date is when you find out if your personalities click. Leave some mystery. Remember that you are in a Ferrari going at a slower pace than usual to prevent mishaps while also seeing what's happening on the other side (of the table, that is). A first date usually lasts about two to three hours, and if it goes longer than that go with your gut feeling. I know that in business you usually leave the other person wanting more. It's like those television series. At the end of the year the series will end with a cliff hanger to keep you dangling. In other words, you will most likely come back for more. Remember, all these tips are strengthening your line.

Mystery is what is missing in today's age. People know all about you before the first date. They have probably Googled you. During the first meeting keep the topics light. Bring up general topics such as the weather, celebrities, places (vacation spots), civic activities, favorite restaurants and events (rodeo). Please work at avoiding politics, religion, sexual innuendos and negative talk. It is *your* job to leave with a cliff hanger. Remember, you want a second date (or do you?). With each date you will find out more and more about your exciting new catch.

Using open-ended questions instead of close-ended questions is a good way to open up the conversation. Start with, "How do you think those Astros are keeping up a winning streak? What do you think their secret is?" Or, "What was the most exciting adventure you've ever had?" These kinds of questions get people to talk instead of answering "yes" or "no." They will let you give an open-ended response as well. Practicing open-ended questions with friends may help to make you feel more comfortable when on a date.

#3. The third element in this process is finding an inviting fishing spot. Yes, environment is very important. A study recently

illustrated how important the environment is. The study looked at "misattribution," which is attributing an exciting environment to the person you are with. The study had one group of men walk across an unsteady suspension bridge. At the other end of the bridge a woman took a survey. The other group of men walked across a "nonfear-arousing bridge" to get to the same woman, who also took a survey. The men who walked across the fear arousing suspension bridge thought the woman was sexy and wanted to ask her out. The men who walked across the nonfear-arousing bridge thought the woman was average and had no desire to ask her out. And you wonder why when you meet your person at Starbucks it doesn't go anywhere.

What was found is that people associate the heart pounding event with the feeling of love. The same will happen if you give them a warm cup of "something." People will quickly warm up to you without even knowing what you are doing.

You need to find the right fishing spot to get the right person for you. Think "misattribution" to stimulate you to find an exciting atmosphere in which to meet your exceptional someone. *Don't go to a movie* unless the movie is James Bond or some other exciting adventure movie that will bring excitement to the date. If you are going to play a sport, it needs to be fun for both parties and without too much competition. Make sure you ask the other party what they think of the plan. No surprises. You want both of you to feel comfortable. Below are some places that can lead to an exciting time. Remember, they are only suggestions if you are having difficulty coming up with activities that will promote an interesting time.

- Karaoke
- Pottery class
- Swing/country western dancing (lessons)
- Painting/Painting with a twist
- Kite flying
- Go karting
- Race car driving
- Bonfire with marshmallows
- Billiards
- Factory tour
- Rock climbing
- Shooting range
- Quaint café, possibly some quiet jazz
- Romantic restaurant
- Golfing
- Ball game (play or attend)
- Charitable event
- Club event
- Lake (have a rock skipping contest, water-ski)
- Beach (make sand castles, volleyball, surf)
- Dog park
- Zoo
- Paddle boating

- Sailing/speed boating

- Museum

- Biking

- Cycling (tandem)

- Ice skating

- Board games/card games/backgammon/chess

- Tennis

- Ferry ride

- Festival

- Miniature golf

- Water skiing

- Batting cage

- Croquet

- River rafting or tubing

- Badminton

- Ice cream

- Theatre, then a café

- Concert, then a café

- County fair

- Circus

- Observatory

- Hang gliding/Watching hang gliders

- Watching the sunset with a drink

- Aquarium

- Drive in movie

- Paintball
- Water park
- Amusement park
- Horseback riding
- Roller blading
- Hiking in a nature park
- A party
- Fossil hunting
- Disc golf
- Wine tasting
- Bird watching
- High school football games
- High school theatre shows

Now let's move on to:

#4. Appropriate bait. When we talk about bait in fishing it can be all types. Let's focus on the lures. They vary in color, shape, size and texture depending on what you want to catch. Lures mean attraction, enticement, inducement and temptation—everything we want to do to increase the interest of our (hopefully) soon to be mate.

An important question in this segment is to ask yourself what type of person you are looking for. If you want to attract a powerful man that is looking for some action, wear all red or all black and make sure it is skin tight to show off all your curves. I am trying to be funny because color and the way an outfit fits your body matters. Therefore, you need to think about what it is that you are advertising. Think of yourself as being in a job interview without the interrogation. Isn't your attire as important in landing a job as your words? How about your body language?

Clothes

Think about it. What you wear tells a lot about who you are. Remember when you were a teenager and how important it was to express yourself with your clothes? Think of that when you want to attract someone. I've been told that the French can tell if you are an American by how you are dressed (casual wear). They themselves prefer dress clothes. Interesting! So ask yourself what your clothes are saying about you and what you want them to say. Is it, "Come and get me? Hi, I'm interesting."? Or is it, "Go away!"? What do you wear when you rush out to the grocery store or do errands? You never know where you might bump into your new love. My saying is, "Be prepared." It's better to be overdressed than underdressed. At least then if you feel out of place you'll still look great.

Style and color are important. What about accessories? Did you know that women love shoes? For you men out there: Women look at your shoes, which tell them about your taste. If you are not sure what looks good on you, then take a friend when you shop for clothes. Make sure it's a good friend who will tell you the truth. For men I suggest asking a woman friend. For women it should just be someone who knows clothes. Believe me, even the most beautiful models don't look great in everything.

You've heard about accentuating the positive? I believe this to be important in all aspects of your life. For now we are talking about clothes and how they fit your wonderful body. If you have a great derrière, then let your dress or pants hug that area. Now I don't mean "squeeze." Same goes for your chest. For men, a fitted shirt does wonders, and for women a little cleavage goes a long way. However, too much will distract even the nicest of men. Think about what you want to attract. You are thinking "long term."

In fishing, the lures may be flashy or different colors to remind the fish of something alive that it would normally eat. What type of person do you want to attract? In the fish world, shiny silver attracts barracudas and eels. Be careful what you want to attract. This is similar to how humans react. Did you know that when humans see red they think of fire or love? Either way, red is known to raise your heart rate and increase blood pressure. Too much red can be too powerful or overwhelming. The opposite is true for blue. When people see blue they think of the sky or the water and this tends to lower the heart rate and calm them down. This is how powerful colors are.

For little guppies, color can save their lives or help them get their mate. If their colors are too bright they get eaten, and if they are too dull they don't get a mate. The same goes for humans. Did you ever watch one of the Austin Powers movies? What did you think of his clothes? Would he repel you or entice you?

Do you value yourself? Show it with appearance, and say it with action. Be the lighthouse for all those boats that are searching for you. Let your light shine—just not as much as Austin Powers' clothes.

Suggested colors to wear are pink, salmon for men. Pick a pink that looks best on you. Again, ask your friends, the ones who are truthful. You want to be seen, but in a good way. Black may look good, but it may not stand out if everyone in the world is wearing it. However, a black and white combo can look rather striking.

Below are colors recommended for both sexes:

- Pink (salmon for men)
- Blue (royal or cobalt is best)
- Turquoise (it's a mixture of green and blue)
- Teal
- *A touch* of black (skirt or shirt or pants or jacket)
- *A touch* of red on upper part of body (tie, shirt, trim, accessories)
- White (white and black together are usually considered a stylish pair)
- Go to a high-end store and ask an expert what colors looks best together on you

Remember, you want to stand out in a positive way. Not like Austin Powers. Everyone is unique.

5. Patience is a virtue

Patience is important when fishing. Fishermen tell me that fishing is a very relaxing sport. For some, dating is a sport. For most of us it is a challenge to find that perfect person for us. Well, fishermen are looking for that perfect fish, and they will wait patiently until they get it. Sometimes they may go back to the same fishing spot many times before finding the fish they want. In life this would be like going back to the same park to walk, or the same grocery store or pharmacy to shop. People have regular spots they frequent. Be that person who does. Someone may keep seeing you in your regular place and eventually feel comfortable enough to come up and talk to you or vice versa. Think of the show "Cheers" (although I am not encouraging you to frequent a bar).

Taking our time seems to be missing in our world. Today, people want instant gratification from a text, email or phone call. That is one reason why some people enjoy fishing. It slows them down. You can't rush a fish to pick up the bait. Too much too soon may prevent you from being savored and appreciated. "Slow" is a theme in this book that you will be seeing again and again to remind you that slow may be better.

A question many people ask is, "When do I know if that person is right for me?" Only time will tell. The important thing is to be you, to be authentic. Authenticity is something we will talk about later in this book.

How do you know if they are a keeper or if they are a throw back? How long do you hold them until you know to throw them back? Just like a fish, if you choose to keep someone too long, they may start to smell. The fisherman who catches a fish that has already been tagged by the wildlife department is told that the fish cannot be kept. It cannot be kept no matter how much of a prize it might be. Well, let's just say the fisherman kept it anyway. Then there may be consequences, as learned in the "no have to's" principle. How does that apply to dating? You may have just snagged the catch of your dreams, but your catch is already committed to another. Sometimes you see this with a ring on the hand or you may hear it in the conversation. This is what is called a "red flag." This is when listening is crucial.

Believe it or not, men and women want the same thing. No, it is not sex. Well, maybe later. Men and women both want "love, understanding and companionship." But love takes time. When you meet someone who you want to be friends with or do business with, how long does it take you to trust that person? A day, a week, a month or a year? It depends on the person and how often you see them. What is the difference if you meet someone you are passionate about? Could it be that there is a sexual attraction? For some reason, when we meet a person for business or as a friend, we do not rush it. We usually fit them into our schedule. We slowly get to know them until we trust them as a business partner or friend.

So what happens when it is someone we are sexually attracted to? What changes? SEX. Yes, that's right, everything becomes more sensual. Suddenly, there is a sexual attraction, and we need to say, "Whoa Nelly!" to slow us down and to let us think what we really want. This is important to remember: Even though you are sexually attracted to a person, it is still going to take a while to get to know them. You may feel as though you have known them your whole life. I am here to tell you that you haven't.

This is when I tell my clients to pretend that they are driving their Ferrari. How about a red hot Ferrari? Let's say you are going 200 mph down the 610 Loop in Houston. You're feeling powerful, sexy, getting a rush and having fun doing it. What could happen? Well, you could run into someone or something or be stopped by a police car. In other words, going too fast could get you in trouble or make you hurt yourself or someone else. Do you want to crash and burn? We are speaking about boundaries here, which will be discussed later in this book.

When you are speeding down the highway, what could you be missing? Is your view a blur? Now take that throttle and pull it back and slow down a bit, maybe to 60 mph. What do you see now? You probably see a lot more than you did before. Now you probably see the scenery much more clearly. It's not a blur. That's what we are talking about in relationships when they first begin. If you slow down your speed and go slower than you have in previous relationships, then you may be able to see repeated patterns in you and in others that weren't working for you, such as picking people who are emotionally absent, or people that put you second. By increasing your awareness you may be able to eliminate some of these patterns or adjust them to become more "aligned," making for a smoother ride.

Bempathy Tip:

Connect *with yourself to find out what "elevator pitch" is* **comfortable** *for you so you will feel comfortable when first meeting your special person.*

CHAPTER 6

Rubbernecking

Where do you find the right person for you? Right beside you? Or maybe at the grocery store? Yep, that's right. A dear friend of mine met her husband while waiting in line at Eatzi's. There is no longer an Eatzi's in Houston, but their love is still going strong. Eatzi's even catered their wedding a few years back. Another friend met his wife at Babies "R" Us, where she worked as a cashier. You just never know where your love will pop up. Just by increasing your awareness of your environment, you can increase your chances of a "close encounter." Rubbernecking is one way of attracting that person into your life.

What do you think of when I say "rubbernecking"? If you live in Houston, Texas, you might think of our wonderful traffic. You might think of people slowing down to look at an accident on the other side of the highway. You might even say a few choice words to the people doing it. Rubbernecking might cause you frustration as it slows the pace of traffic.

Rubbernecking was even sung about in a famous song by none other than that sexy, twisting singer called Elvis Presley. He knew what he was talking about. In his song, he sings, "Stop, look and listen." Isn't this what we want our person of interest to do?

What we are talking about in this book is more of what Elvis was talking about. Now I know it is a little more difficult to stand out in today's age competing with influencers and technology, with people constantly looking down at their phones and all that. But rubbernecking is another way to take action and control in finding the right person for you in your environment. This means having fun doing something unique and eye catching in a positive way— something that makes the other person "stop, look and listen" to what you are doing.

How many people do you know who slow down to take a look at a billboard, especially if it has something offbeat to catch the eye? That can be rubbernecking. Think of yourself as an ad, an eye-catching ad. What are you advertising? Sex, a long-term relationship, independence, intelligence? Think about what your appearance is telling others.

Every time you leave your house, think of yourself as going on an interview or on a first date. This chapter will help you stand out—not like Austin Powers but more like Oprah or Jacqueline Onassis or George Clooney. We touched on some of this in Chapter 5.

A middle-aged man I recently met said that he was told he was "too laid back" and old. I found him to be charming and intelligent but wearing "old type" clothes. Just because you're not 30 doesn't mean you have to dress like you aren't. Remember my "no have to's" principle? I will continually go back to that concept because "have to's" cause us as humans to become "contained" with few options, whereas in fact our options are limitless, no matter what age we are. I have found in both men and women that people don't always wear what looks best on them but what may be in style or what they *think* looks good.

Women look for style and colors on men, and men look for whatever makes a woman look like she has an hourglass figure. We are talking about perception. Believe it or not, that does not mean skinny. Accentuate the positive and remember what attracts those "fish." They are all different. What may attract one may not attract the other. What kind of person do you want to attract? Let's continue our journey by taking a ride in our CABS and seeing where it takes us on our journey to fun and excitement.

Rubbernecking consists of CABS:

- Clothes (color/style)
- Action
- Body (body language)
- Smell

Let's take our CABS and go for a drive. We may pick up the hitchhiker of our dreams. Let's start with clothes insofar as an appealing wrap entices people to want that present. When we wear something that we feel good in our confidence goes up. That's what we want—to entice, to attract and have fun doing it.

Clothes

To be noticed in a positive light, wear fitted and stylish clothes (that look good on you). Studies have shown that the face reflects the clothes. Style has a subliminal effect upon the appearance of physical features. Just look at what George Clooney or Duchess Kate are wearing. When you wear an outfit, ask yourself if George would wear the same or if Oprah would wear the same. Clothes consist of shoes, accessories and the clothes themselves. You don't just wrap a shirt in wrapping paper. You put it in a box with tissue paper. Then you may scotch tape it. Then you may wrap it with a pretty wrap and possibly put a ribbon around it with a bow. Think "total package." Ask yourself if what you are wearing is "with it," in style. And how does it look on your physique? Is it too youthful or too old looking? Does it emphasize the positive? Below are suggestions on how to accentuate the positive:

1. Smile (whiten your teeth)
2. Women: think "sweet, sexy and stylish"
3. Men: think "sharp, sophisticated and stylish"
4. Undergarments (body shapers, lifting bras, think "no lines" [for underwear])
5. Updated styles (take this time and have fun shopping for a new wardrobe)
6. Fitted to flatter (not tight) (trousers/slacks/pants/dresses/skirts)
7. Trendy (depending on your age, not too youthful; ask people at the store what they think)

8. Accessories and make up (remember, less is more)
9. Update glasses (glasses are in now)
10. Shoes (do they match what you are wearing, and are they stylish?)
11. Hair color and style (men love long hair and women love style)

    Women: longer is better; wilder/out of bed look
    Men: stylish, youthful
12. Eyebrows (any hair on face), get it trimmed, shaped or removed
13. If you have gray, there is nothing wrong with a little touch up
14. It is better to be overdressed than underdressed
15. Look at magazines for men and women to see what's "in the now"

Homework:

- Look and see what's in *Vanity Fair/GQ/People/Town & Country/Style*
- Check with retailers for latest styles

Color

You will do the picking of who you will go out with. This section is mainly to get you to "stop, look and listen" so that you *can* do the picking. You have choices.

Color is also talked about in Chapter 5. We are adding it in this chapter because color is extremely important. Think of advertisements. What attracts you to them? *Color* is usually what makes you look at most ads. Think of yourself as an ad. Aren't you advertising for yourself? What colors entice you in an ad? What intrigues you? How would those colors look on you?

Color is so influential that it affects us physically and mentally, speeding or slowing down our heart rate. Too slow or too fast is not what we want when we want to be noticed. Think of Goldilocks. Remember the tale, "Goldilocks and the Three Bears?" Goldilocks is lost in the forest and stumbles upon the bears' house, which has chairs, porridge and beds. Goldilocks was particular about what kind of chair she sat in, what kind of porridge she ate and what kind of bed she slept in. She wanted them all to be "just right." Not too hard, not too soft, not too hot, not too cold, but "just right."

The "Goldilocks Theory" is something that will help to keep you balanced. We want something to be "just right." When wearing colors, it matters how well you match them and what color surrounds your face. When people first look at a person they look at the entire person, then they look at the face.

Want to get seen? Think "peacock." This is your chance to spread that beautiful colorful tail. Take your time and spend some time on this. You have probably been told that your colors are either winter or summer colors. Or that you look good in pastels. We are talking about colors that attract a partner. What are the colors of a beautiful peacock? They are bright colors—gold, royal blue, cobalt blue . . . .

Peacocks and peahens think as Goldilocks thinks. Bigger isn't always better, as far as peahens are concerned. Females may reject males with too much of a good thing. Tails that are too big or too flashy may drive potential mates toward more modest males. This is something to think about in anything you do.

All women look good in some type of pink. Find a pink that looks good on you. Fuchsia looks good on people with darker skin, and peachy pink looks good on most everyone. A study has shown that if you want to win an argument, you should wear pink. When you wear pink you may find that people will treat you much nicer. They will definitely notice you more (in a good way). There are many different shades. Find the one that works for you. Men: That is salmon color for you. You can wear it as a tie or shirt. I would not recommend it as pants. Gray-haired individuals look great in camel color. Maybe a camel-colored jacket and pants with a navy-blue shirt. If it is cold, possibly a hounds-tooth pattern scarf.

People, especially women, tend to wear a lot of black when they want to attract their special someone. Nevertheless, wearing *all* black is not recommended for attracting people. Black is a very powerful color, but you might still not stand out if everyone else in the room is wearing black. Yes, because black is a powerful color you will look sexy. But we are not talking about looking sexy. We are talking about rubbernecking, *standing out in a crowd in a positive way.* Especially nowadays, with most people looking down at their phones, you need to be more enticing than those awesome devices. Not only are we competing with other people, we are competing with technology.

If you feel good in your outfit, it will show. Combinations and color are important. It is also important to get a second opinion. You can buy a book in which it says that this item looks good on that person, but that person might not be you. We are all unique, and that is why you should ask someone who works in a high-end store for a second opinion. They are there to sell and make you look good so that you will want to come back and spend more money.

Ask yourself, "Am I more fun, more interesting and more enticing than technology?" If not, then what would it take? This question is something to think about when you want to grab the attention of people in today's world. Studies have shown that red is thought to make both men and women look more attractive. The color red also raises your heart rate and blood pressure. Therefore, if you are an older man who is laid back and wants to be perceived as younger and more exciting, then red needs to be in your repertoire. Maybe a touch around the face or on a tie. If you are a woman, a bold red necklace with matching shoes may make your face look more exciting. A red jacket will definitely get you noticed – even a touch of red lipstick. But too much red doesn't fit our Goldilocks Theory.

It is important to think about who you want to attract. Women who wear all black or all red will tend to attract powerful men that may be flirty. Black and red when used in moderation as an accent do well. Too much of these colors may be overpowering for people. It also depends on your personality. Red does make you stand out, but you may stand out too much. Remember, we are thinking of Goldilocks and standing out "just right." If you do decide to wear black, make it a skirt or pants, so that your top is something that stands out in a crowd. You want to get people to "stop, look and listen."

You are unique, and it is important for you to recognize that some colors look better on some people than on others, as stated below. Try on the suggested colors mentioned in this book, and ask a clerk how they look on you.

1. Older people or people with a light complexion (think soft and light)
2. Dark hair: can wear most colors (think bright and light)
3. Blue eyes: blue shirts (royal blue is the best)
4. Gray hair: white/gray/black combination can be really sharp
5. See Chapter 5 for other colors that stand out and are liked
6. Increase awareness of what colors entice you
7. Learn what colors look best on you by asking experts in the field

Body

The body is so important. We all are different shapes and sizes. Vive la différence! I have always heard that you should treat your body like a temple. How do you treat your body? The better you treat it, the better you will feel mentally and physically. You will exude confidence in your walk and your stance. Let me ask you a question: Do you want to improve, tighten and strengthen your stance? Do you want to have more energy? If you answered yes, then you may want to think about fitting exercise into your life. If you are not exercising, now is the time to find a way to fit it into your life. If you have medical issues or have not exercised in a while, ask your doctor before starting a program. Exercise will improve your movements and increase muscle strength, muscle memory and metabolism. Below are two elements that improve with exercise and contribute to building your confidence and improving your mood.

- *Gait:* Your gait tells a lot about who you are. Think about how you walk when you are confident. You want to attract people. Think about how Dwayne Johnson walks or anyone else in power. Do they slouch or slump and shuffle their feet? Or do they take long powerful steps? Think Duchess Kate.

- **Posture:** Want to look five pounds thinner? Stand up straight (not rigid). Great posture makes you look taller and five pounds thinner. Not only does it make you look confident, it makes you feel confident. It is even known to improve your mood.

Approachable? Are you?

How do you know if someone is approachable? How can you make yourself more approachable? Are your arms crossed? Are you looking down? Are you smiling? These are things to ask yourself every time you leave your house.

If you want to know if someone is approachable, smile at them. If they smile back they are approachable. It doesn't mean that they are interested, but it does mean that if you say "hi" and use your elevator pitch they will be responsive. You can then go from there. Below are some cues to help you tell if someone is approachable and possibly interested.

1. Eye contact
2. Double take with a smile
3. Slight tilt of the head
4. Arms and hands open
5. Feet slightly less than six inches apart and slightly turned in
6. Leaning forward when you are talking
7. Smiling

Want to feel and look more powerful? Power equals confidence, which equals sex appeal. Recent research proposes that powerful posture along with a slight tilt of the head or a turn of the nose (slightly up) triggers a biochemical reaction in the body that makes you feel more powerful. Doing some of the steps below will increase your confidence.

1. Erect posture
2. Lengthening spine and lifting chin ever so slightly
3. Weight evenly balanced on both feet firmly (grounded)
4. Hands resting lightly on your hips

Increasing awareness of your body and changing how you use it can change your life and improve your chances of meeting the perfect person for you. The way we stand and walk affects our stress level, mood and self-esteem. For example, if you want to decrease your anger, just recline in a chair. Want to feel more powerful and at the same time decrease stress levels? Obtain an "expansive pose." Physically expand your space. That's right, studies have shown that your body stance affects the way you feel about yourself. The world will seem better and brighter, and people around you will gravitate toward you. So start adopting an expansive posture that fits you.

Think of being at a party. You hear laughter and notice someone who is with others, all of them having a blast. What do you want to do? Gravitate towards the laughter. That's what we are talking about in rubbernecking.

Body language can be intoxicating. You've heard the saying, "Some people are bigger than life"? What that means is that they exhibit charisma. You can too, just by following some of these suggestions. Remember, these are only suggestions, not rules. Some of them may work for you, and some may not. You use what you are comfortable with. At first it may feel "not you." Give it a chance. Anything new may feel awkward at first. Practicing this new body language will help to make it part of the new you.

Right now, stand up. Yes, stand up and bow your head, slouch over and shuffle a few steps. After a moment, lift your head in the way we have talked about in the above section. Stand erect, with a lift of the chin and with determination. Strong, slow and steady. Which posture feels better to you? Most likely it was when you stood erect and showed your magnificent face so that the world could see it.

Where you stand in a room and how you stand will increase attention from others. Standing in the middle of the room, erect with your feet six inches apart will help you be noticed. When at the bar, keep your back facing the bar and stand at one end. We are talking about your presence.

"Presence is everything."

How many people do you know who may look average (whatever that is) yet are usually surrounded by adoring fans. It is presence! Think about it. When you are sitting for an interview and the interviewer has a chair that is higher than you, how does that make you feel? Position and presence are important.

97

Studies have shown that the body can show more than the face. Studies ranging back to the 1930s show the importance of the position of the hips. The "hip move" is so powerful it can intimidate as well as tell someone you are interested. I use it when I am counseling. I face both chairs turned slightly toward my desk. I seat myself in one of the turned chairs and the client in the other, causing our hips to be slightly turned away from each other (which is non-confrontational). Our heads still face each other in a non-confrontational way. This tends to make the client feel more comfortable and the talk easier. People don't even realize that we are using the "hip move."

You can even use this move to see if someone likes you. If you turn your hips away from the person you are talking to and the other person turns their hips toward you, that's telling you that the person is possibly interested in what you have to say. It's the same for if they mirror you. If you put your hands on your hips and then they do the same, you can think of it as a compliment. Body language is so important in communication. Some of us do it better than others. It doesn't mean you can't learn how to make it work for you. You can!

The same goes for when you meet people. When you walk up to someone, make sure that your gait is strong and steady but not too fast. Slow and steady is best. When people get excited or nervous they tend to rush things. This is a time to slow it down a bit. Nice and easy does it every time. Take strong, slow, stable steps toward your potential date, keeping at least an arm's distance away. To prevent confrontation, when you reach the person make sure that your hips are not directly facing them. In other words, your hips should be almost directly facing them but with a very slight turn away. Do the same when you are sitting across the table from the person. Position yourself diagonally, or just turn your hips ever so slightly to one side.

Want to feel and look more powerful? Power equals confidence, which equals sex appeal. Take an expansive pose, spread-out but not too much. The more space you take up, the more powerful you look. You want to send signals that you are both confident and unpretentious. Think of little Goldilocks and how she wanted what was "just right." In other words, feet should not be more than about six inches apart. Turning your toes in a little gives you an approachable stance. Voice is important to reeling in both sexes. The tone, pitch and speed in which we talk is important. Research has shown that a nice low voice for both sexes is considered a positive. So listen to your pitch. You may want to slow it down or lower it.

When sitting:

- Maintain eye contact by looking (not staring) at eyes or forehead
- Keep hands and arms open
- Minimal gestures (for fidgeters, hands under a table if possible)

- Think elbows on the arms of your chair
- Lean forward
- Voice low and slow
- Avoid touching your face (even though it may feel good)
- Smile (be real)

When walking:

- Assertive posture (Google a picture)
- Keep head level
- Eyes straight ahead (grazing the room)
- Slow and steady
- Smile

When standing:

- Think: where can I be seen?
- Stand in the middle of the room
- If at a bar stand at the end and have your back to the bar
- Have hands where they can be seen
- Make sure your hands are loose, maybe placed on a chair
- Eyes: browse the room (refrain from staring)
- Feet about six inches apart with toes turned slightly in
- Smile

Smile

People love smiles. No matter if you are sitting, walking or standing, find something to smile about. Did you know that a smile is contagious? Yep. Smile at someone and see what happens. Think about Princess Diana and her smile. She used her eyes with a sweet smile that said, "I am approachable." That is what you want. Please make it real. When people genuinely smile, their eyes smile too. Yes, the eyes crinkle at the corners. Show some teeth. Think of something funny so that your smile will be real. Being authentic shines through and attracts people who are doing the same. Isn't that what you want? Women may want to give a sideways glance. This would be a quick bold look while lowering the head with a slight tilt away. Think Princess Diana. Google a picture of her smiling and greeting people to help see what we are talking about.

Eyes

Yes, the eyes have it. Both men and women use them in the mating dance. Or should I say "dating dance"? Think about it. You are in a crowd of people, maybe a hundred in the room. You see that person at the far end. Wow, your heart skips a beat. What do you do? Run! No, use your eyes. Everyone knows what a "double take" means. It means, "I want to get to know you better."

When you see someone of interest, look at that person as if he or she is your favorite dessert and you want to savor it. Instead of staring at your dessert, look for a second or two and then look away. Of course you need to take another quick look at this delicious morsel. What about your eyebrows when looking? Do you ever raise them? When a person raises both at the same time it means they are interested. Do it with the Princess Diana smile or the George Clooney smile. There you have it. Use those eyes!

Give people space

When meeting someone, remember to keep your space. In our society three to six feet is comfortable for most people. You will know if you have overstepped your boundary if the other person moves back, puts their hand out to say stop, or makes a face. Think of being in line at Starbucks. How comfortable is comfortable? The distance may vary depending upon the person. Maintaining your distance will leave both parties comfortable. This is what you are looking for—comfort. Mirror work will help you realize how to present yourself and feel more comfortable.

Mirror work

- Practice your stance and facial expressions by walking in front of a long mirror.
- Pretend that the mirror is the person of interest and respond to the mirror.
- How do you look?

- Would you approach you?
- Write a dialogue for the person whom you desire to attract.
- Talk to the mirror using your newly written dialogue.
- Are your facial expressions inviting while you talk?
- Do you look and act approachable?

Action

We are talking rubbernecking. What type of action will get people to "stop, look and listen" in a positive way? This is something for you to think about when you are out and about. You want to do an activity that will increase curiosity yet make you approachable. You want the activity to stand out from the crowd in a positive way. Below are some examples of what I am talking about:

- Taking a camera with you and taking pictures of who you are with or the area
- Sitting at a bar doing some interesting work: design, graphics, engineering, writing
- Looking as if you are looking for someone
- Laughing passionately with others (think approachable)
- Walking your dog
- When shopping for cologne or perfume asking bystanders what they think
- In a sports bar asking bystanders sports questions (wearing a shirt with a sports saying)

- Wearing T shirts with sayings on them that make people say, "mmm"
- Doing an action that makes you approachable, not scary
- Going to trendy restaurants where the tables are seated close together
- Asking for help (people get a boost of serotonin [a feel good drug] when helping)
- Doing a good deed, opening the door, giving someone your chair, etc.

Smell

Did you know that most men love the smell of vanilla? Some even like citrus. What do you think of when you smell honeysuckle? Does it make you smile? Do you think of summer or spring? Smell is one of our senses that run on automatic. We may not even know how it is affecting us.

Similar to how we talked before about misattribution, people will mis/attribute smell to you. Therefore, please go someplace that smells good. Think of a restaurant. If it smells bad to you, are you going to eat there and pick out some food? Probably not. So ask yourself, "Do I smell good enough to make someone's mouth water?" Well, do you smell good enough? A good way to find out is by asking a friend—a very close friend, that is.

When you work out, it is important to shower first. Maybe even use Dial soap to get rid of all the bacteria. Okay, that sounds backwards—we should shower after a workout as well of course—but we are talking about smelling good and enticing our soon to be partner. Our body aroma just by itself is enticing to others. Notice I said "body aroma," not body odors! That's because you need to think *fragrance, perfume, aftershave.* You want to create a scent that is remembered in a positive way, a scent that is subtle and enticing. That is what some hotels and offices do. It's so subtle that you may not even notice.

We are unique and so is our smell. Now if you want to spice it up a bit with a perfume or cologne I recommend using a popular fragrance and then asking people how it smells on you. All fragrances smell different on different people.

Subtlety is key. You want to make people feel welcomed, not repelled. Think "approachable." That goes with everything you do. I can tell you what cologne or perfume to buy, but it might not necessarily work for you. Remember that when a friend says, "I use so and so." It is just a recommendation. You need to test the products that you choose. Have fun with them and ask people in the store, preferably someone of interest. You never know if they could be the one. This is a type of rubbernecking. Stand out by asserting yourself and asking people in the store what they think. It might get them to "stop, look and listen."

Rubbernecking is something that Houstonians know a lot about. The above paragraphs described a different twist to rubbernecking. It should put a smile on your face instead of causing you tension. When you walk out of your house ask yourself, "What will get someone to "stop, look and listen" to me (and that is not too outrageous)?"

CHAPTER 7

Internet and App Dating

Dating has gotten lost in translation with our excessive use of technology. Yes, technology is important, yet its constant advancement along with humans' curiosity has caused it to sometimes get in the way of dating.

People are texting instead of talking, which is making them better at texting but not at talking. You should see some people go at it when texting. I have never seen thumbs move so fast. I on the other hand find it quicker just to make that call, say what I want to say, hear the other person's comments and hang up. It takes maybe three minutes, whereas when I text, I keep going back and forth. It can quickly become confusing. By the time I get to the conclusion, I've forgotten what I started with.

I'm perplexed when people tell me that texting sometimes begets confusion and that they end up in a fight. When asked, "How come you don't pick up the phone?" they say that it takes too much energy. What does that mean? In actuality, it is quicker to have a verbal conversation than texting and probably a lot less confusing.

First and foremost, technology is here to stay. It is a necessity, or is it? We have had technology since I can remember. I wasn't born then (I am old, but not that old), but isn't the making of the wheel technology? Technology means "know how." Therefore, it will always and forever be changing, expanding and growing. The problem isn't so much technology; it's that technology has become 24/7. As far as I know, we are not able to keep going like the Energizer Bunny. Humans need to stop and take a break. That is where the problem lies. When is the right time to take a break from your phone, computer, laptop, tablet, Game Boy, etc.? When is the time to use your technology? Does it help in bettering relationships, or does it hinder?

These are questions to think about. People tend to come in and complain that texting and social media have caused problems in their relationships. Sometimes they will talk about meeting someone and say they have been talking to them all week. When asked if they were texting or verbally talking, you know what they say? They say they were texting. The difference between texting and talking is that texting is for connecting and verbal talking is for conversing. Think about it. Texting is good for statements or quick questions such as, "Are you running late?" or "I love you." It is important to remember that most communication with humans is through body language. Texting is "two dimensional," and people are "three dimensional." At least they were the last time I looked.

This chapter is about knowing how to use the internet for dating. There is a need for awareness of how technology is affecting relationships. There is also a need for awareness of the appropriate use of technology. Technology at times may become rude and invasive. People may use technology in avoidance behavior or aggressive behavior. If they are bored with the person they are with, then they may just start to text someone else on the phone. Some people may take pictures of people they do not know and put these "funny" pictures on the internet without the person's permission. Internet dating needs to bring cohesiveness, not invasiveness. The question is: How do you do that in this society we live in, in which technology is 24/7? Below are some helpful suggestions to assist you in making others feel more comfortable and safe.

Texting

Do:

Texting is for connecting, which is a part of communicating. What is meant by "connecting"? Connecting is best used for messages such as short statements or quick questions such as the following:

- Letting someone know that you are on your way
- Letting someone know that you are running late
- Letting someone know the time and place of a meeting
- A love message such as "smack," "hugs," or an endearing name
- Reminding someone to listen to your voice message
- Letting them know you are busy and will call them later
- Use emojis to help set a tone

<u>Don't do</u>:

Keep this in mind when you text: It is a great way to connect quickly while busy doing other things. What you do not want to text are long intricate messages such as the following:

- Making a date
- Conversing back and forth more than two times
- Messaging to get to know someone
- Breaking up
- Arguing
- Discussing
- More than two sentences

The above can cause confusion. People have been known to get into fights because they forgot to include an emoticon. As mentioned before, connecting is a *part* of communicating. Texting may get you from point A to point B. The question is: What do you do after you get to point B?

Because of technology, dating has become easier yet harder at the same time. In essence, technology has given us easy access to people and so many to choose from. There may be too many to choose from. Think about your dating situation. If you are using websites or apps, how many sites are you on? How many sites are out there in cyberspace? Are there other places to meet people through technology? Sure, how about all those chat rooms out there? Or how about playing games online with other people in cyberspace? The problem is that there are so many two-dimensional people hiding behind a screen. It has become too easy, or has it? The screen has turned into a mask. The screen may mask who and what others are. You have heard of catfishing because it has been mentioned earlier in this book. Basically, it has become okay for people to be who they are not.

In the past, when we first saw people we would put on a mask, so to speak. Now we don't need to because we can hide behind a screen in cyberspace. Ways to unmask people on the apps and internet are to:

1. Have an appropriate profile on the dating app or website (we will get to this later in the chapter)
2. Talk on the phone as soon as possible
3. Meet the person in a safe environment
4. Ask pertinent questions on the first date (without interrogating)
5. Go slow, much slower than if you had first met them outside the virtual world

This does not guarantee that you won't still be faked out, but it will help. Even in the "real" world people sometimes wear a mask when they first meet you. My suggestion is to literally sit back and look. Yes, really look at what is in front of you. At first you may see this sexy awesome creature, but upon a closer look you may see something different. Remember that most of us want to make a great impression and will do whatever it takes to look good. So "stop, look and listen." Really hear what the other person is saying and think, "Is this what I am looking for?"

You are the prize, precious and rare. You are the one in control of whom you are with, so choose wisely and slowly. What's the rush?

How to attract that perfect person for you? The first step is to create a wonderful profile, one that is hard to resist. An amazing profile doesn't assure you of immediately getting that special someone, but it will certainly help.

The key to a successful profile is to make it attractive. You can look at some other profiles to see both your competition and what is attractive. You may ask yourself, "What have I done that's interesting? Where do I see myself in five years? How much time a day do I want to spend on the internet or apps?" Finally, ask yourself, "What would make my profile stand out and attract the perfect person for me?"

1. *Goal:* What is your goal? Is it to get as many partners as you can, or is it to have a committed relationship? Before you start writing and composing your profile you need to know what kind of fish you want to catch and what type of relationship you want to have. Only then can you put the right bait out there. If you put worms on your hook, you

may not get that sailfish you have always dreamed of. Something to think about.

2. **_Pictures:_** Think "eye-catching" (in a positive way). Pictures catch people's eyes. Ask yourself, "Whose eyes do I want to catch?" Individuals are attracted to pictures. Think "high quality." Some phones do a good job. Don't Photoshop, be real. Keep in mind that you may eventually meet in person. What and who do you want to attract? You want your picture to attract the kind of person that you are looking for. If you are looking to have a wild time, then be sure to show a lot of skin. If you want to attract someone who is thinking of a serious relationship, think "sophisticated and sexy." Post about three pictures of yourself. Don't include your child or friends. Don't post a picture from which someone has obviously been cut out. This picture is about you, and you need to make it as least confusing as possible.

Here are some suggestions for your three pictures: Picture #1. Your main picture should be a head shot with soft lighting (not touched up), preferably professionally taken. Remember, if you want to catch "real" you need to be "real." Like attracts like. Think, "I want a picture that will express the type of person I want to attract." Please smile. Try wearing royal blue if you are a man and pink if you are a woman. Picture #2. Have this be a full-length picture so that people will know what they are getting. Your potential match is eventually going to see all of you, so start now by showing all of you in the virtual world. Women might try wearing a pink dress (the tint that makes you look the best), sitting comfortably on the couch at home with shoes off, and tilting the head to the side and smiling. This is just an example. Men might try wearing a royal blue button-down shirt with pants and sitting relaxed in the home or office, showing good posture with a very slight head tilt and a smile. When taking these pictures you need to feel comfortable. However you feel will show up in the photos. Picture #3. This should be an action picture. The goal of this picture is to entice people's curiosity. Make it intriguing, not repulsive. Examples would be a travel picture of you in Greece or a picture showing you biking, skeet shooting, roller blading, etc. These are merely suggestions. Try and imagine what type of person will be attracted to these pictures. Is that what you are looking for?

3. *Grammar:* When you read an article and the spelling is wrong or the grammar is off, how does that influence what you think of the author? This is something to think about when writing about yourself in your profile. Also, having someone edit your profile is a good idea. In addition to helping check spelling and grammar, another person can give valuable advice on the content.

4. ***Think resume:*** Make it enticing. Include an eye-catching intro at the very beginning. If it doesn't grasp their attention, no interview! After all, that's what you are after— a personal interview. You want to get the job, but first you need to land the interview. When writing content, think, "Who do I want to attract?" Just as in going for a specific job, you should gear your "resume" to a specific person while still being you (remaining authentic).

5. ***Mystery:*** What has happened to mystery? Research has shown that less is more. Remember, you want to leave them with "wanting more." Think about drinking too much versus going wine tasting. Wine tasting is to get you to buy a bottle. Drinking too much gives you a big headache. Too much information can do the same thing.

6. ***Update frequently:*** Think LinkedIn. Every time you update your LinkedIn profile people get an email saying, figuratively, "Look at me." That's what you want. You want people to look at you (in a positive way). Most dating sites have the same type of formula so that you will show up on search lists. Updating your information every so often by changing pictures or adding some new event that you attended will help you to be seen. You will also look more interesting and exciting.

Meeting people from the virtual world is slightly different (not worse or better, just different) from meeting someone at a party or in the produce department at Kroger. Some people from the virtual world tend to like to and feel more comfortable communicating in a "technological way." This needs to be nipped in the bud in order to encourage a more productive relationship.

You and the people you meet are being taken from a two-dimensional world to a three-dimensional world. This may be a little scary at first because there isn't that time factor in which to write something down, erase it, think about it and edit it. In person, responses are immediate and can't be erased. Oh, no! What to do?

The answer is to go at an even slower speed than you would with someone you meet in person. People that are working in the technological world are used to speed, and we are not talking about the "medication." We are talking about instant gratification. What happens when you don't instantly answer a text or when you wait 24 hours before answering emails? Yes, that's right. People may get anxious and upset.

That is what we are working with. Some people will be looking for instant gratification and thanking you with a text. Therefore, you need to think about how you want this relationship to grow or work for you. Do you want a texting buddy or someone you can physically touch and hear? Modelling the behavior you want will help you get the relationship you are looking for. I emphasize that you need to know what you want, NOT what you don't want.

Talk it over with a friend. Ask them what they are hearing when you tell them what you want. You may be getting exactly what you are asking for without getting what you want and not realizing it. Sometimes we, as humans, send mixed signals.

You can model the behavior you want to get. For instance, on the first date turn your phone off and put it in your purse or pocket. It need not be seen. Your date is the focus for the evening, not your phone. If your date nevertheless picks up their phone, then that tells you what kind of person they are. This phenomenon is called Phubbing - Phone snubbing - which causes disconnect instead of connecting.

Think, "Is this what I want? Someone who puts me second?" This would be a good time to ask them to please put their phone on silent or in their pocket because you want to enjoy the evening with them. If they continue being on the phone or keeping their phone out, then this is possibly a red flag and something to think about.

Promoting conversation:

1. Put all technological devices away and turned off.
2. Dim the lights. Think of your eyes as an extension of the brain. When the lights are on, the brain becomes excited. Research has shown that dimming the lights relaxes people and makes them feel more comfortable.
3. Face your partner. Research has shown that facing your partner encourages social interaction. Just be sure to respect

the hip move by turning your hips slightly away from your partner or by sitting catty-corner. Sitting directly across from each other can feel intimidating.

4. Stay close but not too close. About three to five feet gives enough distance for most people to feel comfortable. If you are too close, people feel invaded, and if you are too far people feel distanced. Adjust your distance as needed.

5. Converse on a cushion. Make sure your chairs are cushioned or padded. Studies show that people are more cooperative on a soft surface.

6. Coffee, tea or me. Have your partner drink something hot. Research has shown that when someone is drinking something warm they warm up to the person they are talking to. So have them hold something warm in their hands for a heartfelt time.

Internet and app dating can be fun, but it is important to realize that a lot of texting and emailing does not mean that you know each other well. Getting to know each other well takes time, and we are talking about face-to-face time.

Whether you meet someone on the internet, through apps, or at a party, whenever you have a hunch about what kind of fit the person might be, write it down to develop your intuition. Make sure to listen to your intuition. Studies show that men and women both have the same amount of intuition (though men may need to increase their awareness of intuition). Sometimes discussing the situation or your hunches with a friend will help keep you from getting off base.

Bempathy Tip:

Empathize *with technology knowing when it is working for us and when it doesn't. Studies have shown putting all electronics away when having face to face* **communication** *promotes* **connectedness.**

Part 2

Your Path to Genuine
Connections Thru Bempathy®

(FOUR EASY STEPS):

B: BOUNDARIES

A: AUTHENTICITY

L: LISTEN

L: LAUGHTER

" Life is a BALL; It just depends on
how high you want to bounce it."

CHAPTER 8

Boundaries

Boundaries. Everyone knows what they are. You've all heard, "Don't put your foot in your mouth." This idiom warns against saying too much, which is the same as overstepping someone's boundaries. Yes, there is such a thing as saying too much. Most of us have been there—in business, with family and friends, etc. Thank goodness my foot is small. How about yours?

This chapter is going to talk about boundaries and how they can help instead of sabotage your relationships. A boundary is a barrier between you and other people. It can be invisible or it can be as physical as your skin. Think of how the Berlin Wall kept people in and kept others out. It both protected and imprisoned. This is what can happen with personal boundaries. Boundaries are different for different people and change depending on the roles people decide to play. For instance, your behavior is probably different towards a friend than towards an employee. Boundaries can fluctuate throughout your life.

Boundaries are the subject of this chapter. But if one chapter isn't enough, feel free to get an entire book on boundaries. There are many out there. This chapter is a beginning that will hopefully get you on the road to a fantastic relationship. We are talking about the relationship that you have always dreamed about.

Let's start with two concepts:

- Less is more. The more you say, the more power you give others.
- Speed limits. Everyone has different speeds. Learn to respect yours and those of others.

Most people do not want to hear your life story. You may think they want to hear all about your previous dates, disasters, marriages, sex partners (if you've had any) and problems. This may surprise you, but people really don't want to hear about that.

It is sort of like rubbernecking. Most people really don't want to see a gross wreck; they are just drawn in out of curiosity. Okay, some people do like gore. I am not one of them. The question is: How do you know when you have said too much?

Do you know? Have you ever put your foot in your mouth? How did you know? What were the signs? Did someone give you a funny look? Did they back away?

This is the reason that I suggest watching for people's speed limits and saying, "less is more" together. Think of yourself as that Ferrari going 200 mph down a highway. You may hit another person or wreck into a tree. If that doesn't happen, you may be stopped by a policeman. Either way, when you go too fast the results are that you may feel hurt, the other person may feel hurt, or you may just get into trouble.

Whatever speed you were going, 20 or 200 mph, slow it down. You will know you are going the right speed for you when your bumps are fewer and the ride is smoother. You may even see things more clearly.

You may be asking yourself, "When should I tell him/her about my past? When should we kiss or have sex?" There are books out there that give specific times for when to do these. I like to say that everyone is unique and that everyone moves forward at different speeds. No speed is "wrong." What is "wrong" is if your speed is not getting you what you want. That is a sign that it may be time for you to slow down. Meeting people - dating is a process to get to know if that person is your potential friend or romantic partner.

1. What is your goal?
2. What do you want?

Someone asked me once, "What is the difference between a pickup and meeting someone?" I think it's something like this: If, after the moment when your eyes first meet and there is that tingle, you both exchange *that* sexual smile, well, then that may possibly be a pickup. If the guy says something like, "Hey baby, you wanna go home with me?" then, yes, it is definitely a pickup. Now, if he says something like, "Hi, my name is John. Would you like to dance?," then this may have some possibilities. The difference between a pickup and a meeting depends on what is said. Or, as a man once told me, "Pickups are fun for a week or so, and the other is a life changing event." Which one are you looking for?

When you meet that special someone, how much do you know about them at first glance? How do they handle life? Where did they come from? What do they do? How long would it take for you to trust them with information? A week, a month, a couple of months? Probably the latter.

How about if you meet a colleague at work where there is not a hint of sexual interest, only friendship? How long would it take to trust them with information about you? Is this different from when you meet someone you want to date? These are thoughts to think about when asking yourself, "When should I have sex with this person?" or "When should I tell them all?"

These questions are even truer when you meet someone from the internet. As someone once told me when I was little: "Stranger Danger." The person could be a spy from another country. How would you know? Okay, let's not get paranoid, but it's important to take the time to get to know someone. People usually have questions on what to do when they first meet. Both parties are usually a little nervous because most of us want to make a great impression. A great saying to think about is:

"What's in it for me?"

This is a saying that is good to think about before you say or do most things on your date. Contrary to what some people believe, this is not a selfish statement. Most things we do in life have some type of payoff. Whether positive or negative, we get something from whatever we do. If you go to work, you get a pay check. If your friend continues to be late at your meetings, you may get frustrated and yell or just not wait for them anymore. Think of consequences before you act. It may help to calm your nerves. For every action there is a reaction or payoff. We are looking for a win/win situation. This is where both parties perceive they are getting a positive "payoff."

My question to you is: "What kind of action/reaction do you want on your dates?" Start practicing the statement, "What's in it for me?" and see if your situation improves. Just keep asking yourself, "Is what I am doing now working for me?" Because if it isn't, it may be time for a detour.

Make "what's in it for me," a win/win situation. Let's talk car dealers. Everyone loves them, right? Well, when buying a car you want to get the best price you can, and you want the dealer to believe he is too, so that you can both get a great deal. You are both saying, "What's in it for me?" Not out loud, but in your head.

That is what is called a win/win situation. "What's in it for me" also helps you maintain healthy boundaries. Before you make a comment or exhibit an action, just think, "What's in it for me to say this? What's in it for me to do this? What's in it for me to be here?" I could go on and on.

People who give too much may want to take a step back, and people who don't give enough may want to think about the consequences of their actions before they do or don't do them. This is where the "slowing down" part comes in. I tell my clients to pretend there is a throttle on the outside of their thigh and to take their hand and move it back in slow motion as if they were pulling back a real throttle. This is to bring them back to the here and now and to help them realize that they might want to slow down. Remember, there may be some curves on this road that you are taking. The slower you go, the better you will grip the road and have a smooth drive. Enjoy the ride.

The first date is the best time to lay down your clear-cut boundaries, before any have been crossed. That is why it is important to know what your boundaries are. Boundaries are different for different situations and for different roles. Basically, you want to be treated with respect and consideration. Think back to your patterns in dating that did not work for you. For instance, calling your date right after the date, being too accommodating, being too available (not having your own life), telling all on the first meeting, getting physical on the third date . . . . I could go on and on. Someone else may do all these things and end up with an awesome relationship. But if you do them and are not getting the relationship you want, then this is where you need to pull back and set some new boundaries that make you feel confident and in control. Only you know what those are. Through practice we learn what is working and what is not. Therefore, ask yourself before you go on that first date where you want your lines to be drawn. What can you tolerate or live with? Let the other person know what is most important to you, such as a monogamous relationship, sexual boundaries, or just staying healthy. You don't have to hand him or her an itinerary or full resume. Remember, communication is more than 50 percent body language. Some researchers say it is more than 60 percent, so watch out for the mixed messages. When sexually attracted to someone our body might be saying "yes, yes," but our mind might be saying "no, no." Conflicting responses need to be resolved in order to exhibit a straight forward message.

When I speak about slowing down, let me clarify. We all have patterns. Some of us might say "Thank you" too much (I have often been told so ☺), or some of us might say "You are so pretty" too much. If so, then slow it down and say it less often. For women: If you're in the habit of inviting a man to an event after only knowing him a month and he doesn't seem to appreciate you, then wait a bit longer before you invite him or don't invite him at all. Every person is unique, and so are your situations. You, however, are the common denominator for your situations. Slow it down and look to see what is working for you (smooth ride) and what is not working for you (bumpy ride or a feeling of swimming upstream against the current). These feelings are your gut saying "mmm." No ride in life is perfectly smooth. All I am saying is that if there are more bumps than not, then it is time to take a different path. Maybe adjust your patterns. Which brings us to the issue of manners. Are they still here, and if not, where did they go?

Manners

What ever happened to manners? I'm probably beginning to sound like your parents. But with today's fast-paced technology, it is often difficult to just say "no." What I mean is that our phones have become an appendage, like our hands or feet. Therefore, when we are on a date we naturally feel the need to attend to our extra appendage. The problem is that in order to make the people we are physically with feel comfortable it is important to give them our full attention. Some of us feel pulled in both directions—the virtual world and the physical world. Which do you want to be in?

Ask yourself this: If after pursuing a job for five years before finally being called in for the interview would you keep your phone out face up on the table? If your phone rang would you answer it during that interview? For that matter, would you even have it on? If you said *yes* to any of these questions, then you really need to read further.

Technology is causing some of our manners to fly out the window. Now I am not talking about etiquette. That is something different and for Emily Post to give advice on. She knew the ins and outs better than anyone. What I am touching on are *manners*. Manners exist to make humans feel comfortable through respect and kindness. Isn't that what a date is about? To feel comfortable and make the other person feel comfortable so that you can get to know them better? Manners have to do with respecting your boundaries and those of others.

Let me ask you some questions: How do you feel when people are talking loudly on their phone at a restaurant when you are eating dinner right next to them? How do you feel when you are in the middle of telling an important story to a friend and they pick up the phone to answer it in the middle of your story? These are just a few questions to make you think of what is appropriate and what is not.

As stated before, everyone is unique. Therefore, everyone's boundaries are going to vary. Not only will they vary because of our uniqueness; they will vary according to the role that we are playing. We play many roles in our lives: sister/brother, aunt/uncle, mom/dad, friend/foe and employee/employer, among others. For each role we are expected to behave a certain way. There I go with the expectations. How are we expected to act with another person when we have this new appendage called *technology*?

Manners are essential to how we relate to a person. For instance, how do you want to relate to *your* date? It's a good idea to treat people as you would want to be treated in that particular situation. Smiling and exchanging pleasantries will encourage the other person to feel comfortable. Do you want that person to do what you want? If so, acting and being warm and positive will inevitably help.

Manners, which are a component of respecting boundaries, appear to be lacking in our society. You see it in everyday life, for instance at a Starbucks when everyone is sitting with friends yet looking down at their phones or working on their computers. This is called Phubbing – look it up. You see it when people are driving while on the phone. You see it with family members when they are texting while at dinner. Where are the manners of the "good old days?" Where have they gone?

Social media has not changed manners. Or has it? Manners are behaviors that show respect and kindness to another person through awareness of the different boundaries present. Okay, that being said, manners are basically a way of showing appreciation of another individual.

Simple courtesy

We are talking about the difference between rushing and bumping around during the day and slowing down and admiring the day. What goes around comes around. The common theme in this entire book is to *slow down*. You never know what you may be missing.

Courtesy, politeness, manners. Do people even know what they mean anymore? Believe it or not, people still prefer to receive a handwritten thank you note instead of an email or (even worse) a text. So yes, courtesy does exist. The question is: When is it important to be polite? The answer is: As often as possible.

Respect, consideration and kindness are still important qualities to have in relationships. You are probably asking yourself what the best way to behave in social situations is. Well, it depends on where and when. The most important thing is to have consideration for the people around you. Instead of walking while texting and possibly bumping into the person in front of you, lift your head up from your devices and look at the world you live and breathe in. That is the first step!

How can anyone have a healthy relationship of any sort if they can't be respectful to friends, family or business peers? Just a thought. When using manners, you will start to find people attracted to you just by your thoughtful acts and a smile. You may even start to notice a change in your attitude and how you feel about you.

Eye contact is extremely important for a couple of reasons: 1) It will prevent a collision, and 2) it lets the other person you are with think you are interested in what they have to say. I say "think" because sometimes people appear to be listening when they aren't.

Looking around or at your phone says "distracted" and "I'm not particularly interested in what you have to say." This could be considered body language; it could also be considered bad manners. Below are some good manners to use when you go on a first date. The first four are recommended if you meet the person from an online site:

1. Exchange two to four texts before talking on the phone.
2. Have two phones (a disposable one for dating).
3. Talk once or twice before meeting.
4. Give your friend the person's screen name, location of the date and how long you expect to be there.
5. Remember, you are strangers, therefore don't mention sex unless that is all you are looking for.
6. Meet in a safe public place where there are a lot of people.

7. Be on time.

8. Dress appropriately (described in previous chapters).

9. Silence your phone and put it away.

10. Make introductions (hello, and your name) with a firm handshake looking the person in the eyes.

11. Say "please" (a great word to use when wanting something).

12. Say "thank you" (use after you receive something).

13. Say "you're welcome" (good to use after someone says "thank you").

14. Say "excuse me/pardon me" (use as an opener to a crowd of people or to excuse yourself from something such as leaving the table).

15. Apologize if you believe you have offended someone or made a mistake.

16. Ask yourself, "What's in it for me?" (before doing or saying anything; this may help with foot in the mouth issues).

17. Don't monopolize (remember, less is more).

18. When talking be aware of your volume and tone.

19. Show interest.

20. Refrain from bragging (behavior speaks louder than words).

21. Make conversation/small talk (keep it light; be prepared to talk about food, exercise, travel, TV shows, etc.).

22. Feel free to throw in a compliment.

23. Remember, alcohol makes for loose lips.

24. Put a time limit on the first date (if the date is good, a time limit leaves you both wanting more; if it doesn't work out you have an excuse to leave early).

25. Don't say you'll call unless you are going to do so.

26. **Men:** Please take the initiative. Remember, this is a first date and you are both strangers to each other. Ask if there are questions: Would you like a drink? Would you like me to order for you? May I get your chair? Etc.

27. Use table manners (you may want to Google this).

28. Please be courteous to the waiter (that shows how you treat others).

29. Hygiene (communicates that you respect yourself and others by not smelling).

30. At the end of the date, if it didn't work out, say, "Thanks so much for meeting me. Have an enjoyable evening."

31. **Men:** Since you are the protector and provider it is suggested that you pay (ask first, "I would like to pay for the meal. Is that okay?").

32. **Men:** Please think about holding the door (ask, "May I get the door for you?").

33. **Men:** You may want to walk the woman to the car for safety.

34. **Men:** You may even offer your arm for stability.

35. **Men:** If you want a second date, ask (a 24-hour wait is suggested; remember, you have a 50 percent chance of success).

36. **Men:** If you don't ask, you have a 100 percent chance of failure.

After the first date, what do you do? Some women and men may not want to hear this, but men provide, protect and are the pursuers. The reason is physical. Men have more testosterone than women, and last time I looked there were some other differences as well. If women would be shot up with testosterone, they would possibly become more aggressive and want to pursue more. Again, this is physical, and there are some exceptions to all this. And again, for women it depends on what you want. All relationships are different.

I myself am the type of woman who likes to be in control. I go after what I want. For some reason that didn't work in my past relationships. So I decided to "slow it down" a bit, and now I am married to a great guy who respects me and brings me flowers. He will be the first to tell you that I think like a guy. So just remember, whoever you are and however you are, look at your previous patterns and ask yourself, "Did they work for me?" If they didn't, either slow down and think before you repeat them or don't repeat them at all.

After the first date, ask yourself how it went. What does your gut feeling tell you? When you have a hunch, write it down to develop your intuition. Listen to your intuition. Go with it. What do you have to lose? You already know you are a wonderful person. You just want someone else to share the wonder. If they decide they don't, then you know you are going to need to continue your search. This is a fantastic adventure. It is open to all possibilities. Have fun on this journey of yours. The more fun you are having, the better chance you may have of finding that fun person to share your life with.

Bempathy Tip:

*When in a situation **communicate** with yourself saying "What's in it for me?" This gets you to be aware of the position you want to be in with the other person which will create **comfortability**, a feeling of **control** so that you can **commit** to continuing the conversation. Remember it is reciprocal in order to make it a win/win.*

CHAPTER 9

Authenticity

Authentic = NOT avoidance behavior

Avoidance behavior = not only not getting to know oneself but not getting to know others

Technology versus authenticity: Is that an issue?

Authenticity or "being yourself" doesn't mean telling all, being the loudest, or burping in front of the President of the United States. What it does mean is being true to yourself and speaking from the heart. In other words, stand by your word. Stand behind your words.

Hold on to some mystery by toning things down and pulling the throttle back. You are still being true to yourself. There is nothing sexier than someone who is comfortable in their own skin. A person who is true to their own personality, essence and character is seen as charismatic. People saying what they mean and sticking by what they say through their actions are seen as trustworthy. Isn't that the type of person you would like to meet? Be that person!

The title of the book says it all: *Meeting People: It's Not a Game*. Sometimes you think people are playing games, and maybe there are some out there that do. Most people who want a relationship of some kind are not playing games. Instead, they may be doing what I call the "push/pull." You've seen these people or possibly dated them. You might even be one yourself. They call frequently, then, when you let yourself go and become available for them, they back off. Then you back off, and back they come. I could go on. You could call it the yo-yo effect. In general, people—both men and women—may act this way if they believe they are getting too close and want to avoid any pain. Therefore they stay far enough away to believe they are in full control. They are engaging in avoidance behavior to avoid pain. Remember, we are attracting who we are with. The more you feel comfortable and secure in your skin, the more you will attract people to your life who feel the same.

When we think of authenticity we think of genuineness. The fourth chapter talks about you being a gift. This is true. Think of yourselves as a "prize," a present to be slowly unwrapped. Finding out who you really are is a lifelong journey. We are talking about being true to yourself so that you can stand up for yourself and be respected. By knowing who you are and believing in yourself you gain confidence, giving you the feel of power and control. Isn't that what we are looking for in life?

In one of his movies, Tom Cruise says, "You complete me." However, that is Hollywood. You may be disappointed in this statement: "No one will complete you." Someone else might accentuate the positive, or you might feel like a better person because of them. But no one will complete you. Work to feel completed before you meet your special someone. That means you are feeling good about who you are and that you know who you are. Chapter 4, "U R a Gift," will help you build confidence. That confidence will flow over onto whomever you are with. Be proud of your awesome imperfections. If you have ten extra pounds or some wrinkles that you believe are an added attraction, others will believe it too. These imperfections are what make us special. They are what make us unique. Want to attract more authentic people? Then be authentic. Think, "the law of attraction." Gain confidence by being authentic.

Authentic:

1. Being true to yourself by being yourself
2. Standing up for yourself (establishing boundaries)
3. Knowing your values and having your behavior match them (consistency)
4. Believing in yourself

What does this mean?

1. *Being true to yourself*

- Accept your awesome imperfections.
- Have your behavior match your beliefs.
- Don't take yourself too seriously.
- Watch out for mixed messages (yours and others').
- Do things that make you feel good about you.
- Accept that you are unique.

- Do one thing for yourself every day (take time for yourself).
- Journal (increases awareness of patterns, feelings and wants).
- Exercise.
- Spirituality.
- Refrain from letting peer pressure influence your decisions.
- Have a healthy support system (support groups) (*Discussed in Chapter 4*).
- Ask for help when needed (take feedback with a grain of salt).
- Have consistency (daily routine).
- Get enough sleep (8/7 hours a night).
- Eat healthy (nutrition).

2. *Standing up for yourself*

When peer pressure finds you,

- Remove self from situation.
- Think of what is right for you.
- Go where the sugar is.
- Remember that you are valuable (a prize).
- Remember that you have choices (thoughts and behaviors).
- Remember you have the right to say "no."

Different ways to say "NO"

1. Maybe
2. Perhaps
3. We'll see
4. It depends
5. Next time maybe
6. I'm not ready (comfortable) at this time
7. It's not my interest
8. I don't know
9. If I get around to it
10. I need to look at my schedule
11. I doubt it
12. I am unable to do it right now
13. I would love to, but I'm just real busy right now
14. I have something else on my agenda right now, maybe later

3. *Knowing your values*

Values vary with each person. Look at your list in Chapter 4. Are you living up to your values? Does your behavior match what you find important in life?

- Honesty
- Family
- Respect
- Loyalty
- Love
- People
- Morals

This is the time to look at the list you made in Chapter 4. And to ask yourself: Does my behavior match my values by at least 80 percent? That's a high mark and will tell you that you are going on the right path (for you).

How do you command respect?

- By how you present yourself
- Trust in your performance
- By how you treat others
- Attire (dress)
- Demeanor
- Attitude
- Hygiene
- Less is more (some people confuse honesty with telling all)

- By how you communicate (verbally and physically)
    1. Voice/inflection/tone
    2. Words
    3. Mixed messages
    4. Your stance
    5. Facial expression

4. Believing in yourself

- Be straight forward
- Be consistent (behavior, thoughts and patterns)
- Stand up for yourself
- Gain self-respect

Emotionally available people may behave showing:

- Affection (emotional intimacy)
- Accountability
- Thoughtfulness
- Gratitude
- Attention to feelings
- Active listening (their behavior speaks louder than words)
- Standing by their word
- Flexibility

- Inclusive behavior

What are your ingredients? Write down who you are. Your beliefs, perceptions and values together will help you to find out who you are. Remember, who you are is your reality. If I believe that I am the most beautiful woman in the world, then I am. That definitely would be my own reality. Well, maybe my husband too.

You can ask friends what type of a person they think you are and apply the information if you believe it fits you. Whatever you write, remember that less is more and that being yourself does not mean telling all or being all you can be. Mystery is a wonderful thing. We are not talking about lying. We are talking about wanting more. Think of those cliff-hangers ending the last episode of television shows in the spring that draw you back to watching those same shows months later. People want mystery. Mystery is enticing. With that in mind, list your ingredients below. How do you define yourself?

_____

_____

_____

_____

_____

Knowing and accepting who you are will help you to become more independent and autonomous. When we think of the word "autonomous" we think:

- independent
- self-directed
- self-sufficient
- free
- self-ruling
- self-governing

My question is: Is anyone truly free? "Autonomous" does not mean that we don't depend on anything or anyone. We do not live on a deserted island all by ourselves. What it does mean is that we are the captain of our ship, the driver of our race car. We have the ability to navigate where we want to go and who we want to be with. We may not be in control of who we are attracted to, but we are in control of who we pick.

If you were in your race car getting ready to race in the Indianapolis 500 (my favorite race), would you sit there and think about who you might hit or what negative thing might happen? Most likely you would not only be envisioning that you finished the race but that you finished as number one. Otherwise, why be in the race? Well, you are in a race to be number one in your life. You are a winner speeding down the road of your life. You are independent, self-directed, and free to handle your race car how you see fit.

Sometimes you may need to slow down to hang onto a curve or you may need to pass a car that gets in your way. You are being autonomous. No one is telling you how fast to go, what car to pass or how to take that turn. That is your decision. That is your concern.

"Autonomous" in a sense means taking responsibility for yourself or your character. It means taking ownership of your actions and intentions. This is great because it gets rid of the word "blame." Blaming ourselves or blaming others can keep us stuck in the past. We want to be able to regulate our control and direction. We don't want to continue to stay in the past by talking about it in a negative light. I have a saying:

"When we bring the past into the present it becomes our future."

Let's keep the past in the past and learn from it and grow. Remember that we are self-directed and self-sufficient and free to choose. We have the choice to be with a certain person or not. Most likely no one makes us date someone. There may be some exceptions. You may think that you should or that you need to date that person, but in reality you are independent and free to choose who you want to be with.

You are the one who chooses. You know you are being authentic and autonomous when your world starts to flow. This is the beginning of you moving down the current of your life at your own speed and finding the fish you want. If they stink, then throw them back. Your stream is full of possibilities. Don't get stuck on a rock. Float over or around it. You are the captain of your ship.

Since we are not an island it is very important to go where the sugar is. Be with people who promote, not suppress you. Start to attract people who encourage, stimulate, foster, support, help, endorse and basically campaign for you. Remember that the law of attraction is working 24/7. You have probably heard the saying, "What goes around comes around." It means: Be that person you are looking for. Be encouraging, be supportive, be motivated to attract and have that relationship that you have always dreamed of. Be your true self, and the sugar will follow. I am not saying there won't be some bumps along the way. You are working on focusing on the sugar. This is when we need our support system to help turn us away from the bumps and toward the sugar. Your support system will remind you of who you are through words and behavior. The point of this chapter is to accept your awesome imperfections while focusing on your gifts, which are to be slowly unwrapped by the person of your choice.

This all sounds so easy, doesn't it? Well, then why are we sometimes sucked into the negativity of our surroundings? Why, after reading that we are autonomous and authentic, do we continue to feel bad when someone doesn't call us when they say they will or when someone says something to us that we don't like?

Unique. That is what we are. Feeling okay about being different is the same as feeling comfortable in our own skin. It will help us to stand up for ourselves and catch those negative thoughts as they pass by. We don't have to change. We are talking about making an adjustment and the consequences of that. If we keep going down the same path, then we will get the same things. What do you want? How would you treat your Ferrari if it were out of alignment and running rough? Wouldn't you want to give it an adjustment so that it ran smoothly?

Notice the red flags. I don't mean just the red flags in other people. Notice the red flags in yourself as well. Some people bring out the best in us and some people bring out the worst. Who do you want to be with? That is the question. Just because someone looks good in ink (or on paper), talks well, is dark and handsome, or tall, blond and sexy, does not mean that they are the person for you.

You want to feel comfortable being yourself. Being yourself doesn't mean showing all of you at once. You want to leave some mystery. Relationships take time. Even though you might think that you have come to know someone faster thanks to technology, I am here to tell you: "You don't!!!"

You've heard that it takes time to heal. Well, it also takes time to get to know someone. All that you are told on a first date are just words. Behavior speaks louder than words. Therefore, "listen" with your ears *and* your eyes.

Listen to yourself as well. Someone once told me they were ready to meet THE ONE—someone who was emotionally available and open. Yet throughout our conversation she kept saying, "I don't feel comfortable sharing emotions." This is why it is important to have a friend or someone listen to what you are saying. Remember, the law of attraction is working 24/7. That's why this person kept attracting men who also did not feel comfortable sharing emotions.

She was giving out a mixed signal—wanting one thing and saying another. This could be considered a red flag. Red flags signal both ways. Remember, people just need adjustments. They don't need to change.

Be that person you want to attract, and remember to appreciate your awesome imperfections. Studies show that people feel more comfortable with a person who appears imperfect than with one who appears to have no flaws.

There is someone out there who will enjoy your loudness, messiness, shyness and the wrinkles in your smile. I could go on and on. It's been said that "there is no such thing as reality, only perception of reality." Being authentic and autonomous is what you make of it. Is it working for you in attracting that special person? If not, then you may want to start listening and looking at your actions and words.

Bempathy Tip:

Banter *and* **empathize** *with yourself so you know who you are so you can better* **connect** *with others by finding* **commonality** *in others.*

CHAPTER 10

Listen

Listening. Is it even important anymore when it comes to communicating in today's world? Do we need to listen? The answer is "Yes." Listening is extremely important and is something that is becoming lost in our society. Think about it. How can you listen to an email or a text? Can you hear the words being said? I don't think so. Can you hear the tone, inflection and pitch? Can you see the facial and body language as you read the print? I think NOT. Listening is becoming a lost art. Yet listening is a big part of communication.

What about listening to your own internal dialogue? Yes, that is part of communication too. Communicating to yourself. Having a smooth relationship with yourself. Remember: if you don't have a good relationship with yourself, then how can you expect to have one with someone else?

Flirting also is a big part of communication. I guess the use of emoticons and even sexting is considered flirting nowadays. Remember those days when you looked across a crowded room and saw that special person? Your heart started to race. Your hands started to quiver. Those suggestive looks from those sensual eyes from across the room. That warm beam of light shooting from their smile. The long uncertain walk to say, "Hi". Hearing their voice for the first time. Wow! Does texting do that for you? We need to ask ourselves if we are still relating, communicating and connecting.

An article in the *Washington Post* a few years back noted that people are breaking up in a text or finding out they are single on social networking sites. What is that telling you? If more than 50 percent of communication is body language (depending on what research you read), then how do you think technology is affecting our intimacy? Is it affecting yours?

This chapter will help you learn to listen so as to see what you might have been missing. You will start to listen to others as well as to yourself. You will start to listen to your inner voice or your intuition when seeing people's cues flash in front of your eyes: their look, their smile, their words, their tone, their movement as they respond to your glance. All this might just be telling you, "I want more."

How thrilling. Meeting people is exciting and can be fun. Sometimes we take ourselves too seriously. Things have become black and white, literally. Think about it. Isn't a text black and white? (Well, *sometimes* other colors are used.) Ask yourself, "Don't I want to put more color back in my life? Well, start looking and listening. Maybe it's time for you to stop and smell those sensual roses. Not the ones that are two-dimensional, but the ones that you can physically touch and see.

People often ask me, "Where can I find the right person for me?" Well, we touched on it in Chapter 5, "Going Fishing." In this chapter we are talking about increasing one's awareness of one's surroundings and seeing the cues. Many people today are caught up and feel more comfortable in the technological (virtual) world. Recently, a man told me about how he had talked to a person he was dating all week long "through text." What do you think of that? Then he became upset when the person he was texting would respond quickly to certain messages and not at all to others.

If people would just pick up the phone and listen. If the person on the other end doesn't pick up, you can leave a message for them to call you back. It would just take a minute of their time. None of this texting back and forth, taking forever and a day to get one message across that may be misunderstood in the end. There are no cues to look for except emoticons. I once put "K" in response to someone's message, and the person on the other end of that two-dimensional world became upset, thinking that I was mad. Apparently, I should have inserted a smiley face after my "K." Now really, all I said was "K." My husband even laughs when I insert a "K," questioning if it is even a word. Is it??

People misinterpret texts, which can cause them to not get another date. Once people have started to date, a particular text message may even cause a fight. What happens when people meet in person? What about body language? People are having difficulty reading body language because they are not practicing it. When people no longer know how to read body cues, they may be misinterpreting what other people are saying without even knowing it. Also, some people may be giving mixed signals by telling others one thing while their bodies are telling them something else. Wow, this is a lot to take in.

Actually, stepping back and looking and listening may make things easier. Below are some examples of what people may possibly be telling you through their body position:

- Crossed arms = uncomfortable/frustrated/defensive or cold
- Biting fingernails/fidgeting/chewing a pen = anxious
- Hands and arms open = I'm open
- Rubbing back of neck = tired, frustrated
- Sitting on the edge of chair and leaning forward = interested
- Smiling = interested/cooperative/open
- Hand on face = avoiding/bored/tired
- Leaning away = defensive/avoiding
- Shoulders back = confident
- Chin up = proud

The purpose of the bullet points above is that listening and looking is more than just listening. It is using your five senses. There are many books about communication. This chapter is to get you to meet and find that genuine connection with someone. That is the goal. Everything takes practice and sometimes too much information, as I have said before, is a drawback. Continue to be you while increasing your awareness of your surroundings and how you affect it. It's just like driving a sexy sports car. If you drive it too fast you may bump into more than you want and may miss seeing some of the beauty that you are passing. So watch your speed.

Listening goes both ways. We are talking about "reciprocal listening." Think of communication as a dance. It is reciprocal, yet someone is taking the lead. If both parties take the lead, what happens? You guessed it. If they were on "Dancing with the Stars," they definitely would not get the 10 they wanted from the judges.

Reciprocal listening means that both parties are "working it." It takes two. Believe it or not, you cannot argue with just yourself. It takes two. If you do decide to argue with yourself, I promise you will always be the winner. Reciprocation is a give and take type of partnership. Isn't that what your goal is? If so, then reciprocal listening will turn out to be a winner.

When we talk about listening, we aren't talking about just "hearing." I hear music, but unless I am listening to the words I won't get the full meaning or the full essence of a great piece of music. The same thing applies to having an awe-inspiring conversation.

That is why this chapter is called "Listen." We humans have five senses. In addition, there is a sixth sense that is called "intuition." So let's just say that we have six senses. We need to increase our awareness of them. First, let's just name them in case you have forgotten what they are. Because of the overuse of technology we seem to not need as many senses as we are blessed with.

So here goes. Let me know if I got it right:

- Smelling
- Sight
- Hearing
- Touching
- Tasting
- Intuition

How did you do? Did you name them before me? If not, then keep reading. You probably have realized by now that throughout this book we have been talking about how our senses affect our relationships. What color you wear, where you stand in a room, how you sit, and what you say all have an effect. Before we go further here is an exercise that may help you to become aware of your senses.

Stop and smell the fruit

1. Take a lemon
2. Close your eyes
3. Feel it and describe out loud what it feels like
4. Smell it and describe out loud what it smells like
5. Open your eyes and describe out loud what you see
6. Taste it and describe out loud what it tastes like

You have just practiced using your five senses and had an intake of Vitamin C while you were at it. Of course, if you're allergic to lemons you can always pick another fruit. The first sense discussed will be smell. We are only going to talk about smell, sight, hearing, touch and intuition.

Smell

I would like to talk about smell first. I know that you have heard of pheromones and what they do. That is not what I am going to talk about. I am going to talk about hygiene. You may not think of hygiene as belonging in the arena of communication, and yet it does. What does body odor tell you about a person? Does it tell you how much they care about their body and health? Smell is quite important in communication. If someone has bad breath, how close and how long will you want to converse with them? This is something to think about when you are out and about. So, how do you know how you smell? Ask a friend! If you are thinking about getting close to someone, physically or emotionally, then remember that smell can be an asset or a disadvantage. When someone has healthy hygiene it lets you know they take good care of themselves and show respect for others.

Sight

Let's touch on sight. When you see someone who is disheveled, what does that make you think of? Unkemptness, uncleanliness, or maybe disorganization? Appearance is part of communicating your self-expression and personality. How many of you have seen someone from across the room and known in a millisecond that you were attracted to them? How many of you have met a person that you were attracted to until they opened their mouth, at which point they became instantly ugly? If you answered yes to either of these last two questions you may be on auto pilot when making these kinds of decisions. You can change that by starting to question yourself.

By questioning yourself I am talking about realizing who and what you are attracted to and who and what you want to end up with. If you are attracted to someone who is compatible with you, great, that means everything's working. If on the other hand you are attracted to someone who is literally driving you crazy, then maybe you need to look at who and what you are attracted to.

Physical attraction is significant and gets people together. But then the complicated stuff begins. People open their mouths and bring their baggage into the dialogue. This is where it's important to watch how a person's body language responds to your words. Their movements will tell you a lot.

If someone physically pulls away or closes their hands or crosses their arms, then that is a possible sign to change the subject.

There is nothing wrong with changing the subject. You are just getting to know each other, and there is no rush to push subject matter. The goal is to establish trust by listening and understanding, not by judging. This may be difficult because people bring along their perceptions and baggage. Therefore, it is important to be as non-judgmental as possible. Look at the other person as someone to have fun with for the evening. Stay in the here and now. Who knows? This may lead to something you have been looking for.

Sometimes we look at a person when we first meet them and say to ourselves, "Mmm, can I see myself with this person in the future?" instead of saying something to the effect of, "I am here to have a fun evening." Stay in the here and now. Be aware of this internal dialogue and how it affects your outcome. Keep the conversation light and breezy with amusing topics that keep you smiling. The expectation is to enjoy yourself.

Visually, smiles are the best. Having a light conversation and looking to the positive will encourage both of you to smile more. Smiles are inviting and comforting. While smiles are important, steady eye contact is too. That does not mean "staring." Intermittently looking away puts people at ease.

Please turn off and put away those phones, or keep them in the car. This date is only one to two hours out of your busy day. Be attentive. Enjoy. To show interest you may lean slightly forward or sideways while sitting. Please don't stay in one position. You don't want to look like a robot. When people are enjoying each other they might begin mirroring each other. That means that when you smile, they smile. When you cross your arms, they cross theirs. Below are bullet points of how you might know if a person is interested:

- Asking questions about you
- Leaning slightly forward
- Mirroring (for example, you turn your waist to one direction and they do the same)
- Tilting their head
- Wanting to be close to you
- A light touch
- Eye contact
- Posture
- Nodding of head (don't be a "bobble head")
- Comments (for example: "Yes. Interesting. Really? Oh? How about that? And then?")
- They are able to remember what you said

The same goes for you. If you are interested, show it. Please remember that less is more. Therefore, time your rendezvous. At the beginning of your meeting you may want to let the other person know that you need to be somewhere in two hours. This will leave you both wanting more. And if the date is not going as expected, then you have an easy way out. Time is precious, and that means for both parties. Putting a time limit on your meeting makes the time you are spending with each other even more valuable.

If you tend to get nervous and fidget, then this may cause the other person to feel uncomfortable. Remember, this is reciprocal and fun. Below are some suggestions to help keep communication positive:

- Refrain from moving your body too much or too little. Think of Goldilocks.
- Refrain from fidgeting (or sit at a table so that you can put your hands and feet under it).
- Refrain from pointing a finger.
- Refrain from wringing your hands.
- Refrain from constantly touching the other person without asking.
- Refrain from touching your face.

Hearing

Hearing is not only hearing the person of interest but also hearing yourself. That means *listening* to your tone, inflection and words, as well as to your internal dialogue and silence. Yes, silence. Haven't you heard that silence is golden? There may be some awkward silences. That is okay. You are meeting this person so that you can understand and get their perspective on life. The question may be, how do you get the other person to open up? By opening up yourself. That doesn't mean telling all or monopolizing the conversation.

A story

If you want to improve communication and motivate the other person to talk, then tell a simple, short, fun story. Think of Joel Olsteen and of how he begins a sermon. He always begins with a short funny story that his audience can relate to. That is what I am talking about. Have a story memorized so that in a moment of silence or awkwardness you are prepared to keep the conversation flowing. This will help to make both of you feel more comfortable.

Use open-ended question to continue to make the conversation flow. Open-ended questions usually start with *how, what, where, who,* or *which.* They encourage the receiver to expand on the discussion. Avoid close-ended questions, which usually start with *is, are, do, did, can, could* or *would.* They encourage the receiver to answer either "yes" or "no." Instead of saying, "Is everything okay?" try asking, "What's going on in your life?" Or, "How are things going?"

What follows are antonyms for listening that might cause roadblocks when you meet someone. These are what NOT to do:

- Dispute
- Ignore
- Refuse
- Reject
- Disregard
- Forget

- Neglect
- Turn away
- Speak to interrupt
- Talk too much

The above words are from *Roget's 21st Century Thesaurus, Third Edition*. Ask yourself if you do any of the above when you meet people. Sure, you talk, but when is the right time to do so? President Lincoln famously said, "Better to keep your mouth closed and be thought a fool than to open it and confirm it." Mark Twain said, "We have the right to freedom of speech and the common sense not to utilize it."

Please avoid using these:

- You
- Why
- But
- Interrogating

"You" and "why" might put people on the defensive, and "but" takes the power away from whatever you said before. A good example is, "You are so beautiful, but that blouse looks awful on you." I like to say that we should sit on our "butts" rather than using the word when speaking with others. Try and use "and" instead. As for interrogating, it's extremely different from interviewing. Just think of a prisoner being interrogated versus being interviewed by

Ellen DeGeneres. Interrogating happens when you appear to be probing, digging for knowledge or information, or applying pressure to get information. Information needs to come willingly from both parties. Think light and breezy. Keep this in mind before you do or say anything: "What's in it for me?" That will help you to think of the consequences of your actions.

Touch

Touch has a power element to it. When you touch someone you are giving yourself power. On the other hand, if you ask someone, "Would you like to take my arm so that I may walk you to the car?" or, "May I give you a kiss?" then this is asking permission, which is showing respect. Some people are touchy feely and love to touch. Others don't want to be touched at all. Either way, it is important to ask first unless you have been dating for a while.

Intuition

This is where past experience comes into play. You are listening and looking at this person sitting in front of you to get to know them. Even though we say we do not judge, it is nevertheless difficult for people to stay in the here and now and not bring along any baggage. We bring our impressions and perceptions to the date. Take this time to take a look at your list of traits that you want in a person, the ones that you wrote down in a previous chapter. Does the person that you are sitting with have most of these traits? Watching how the person of interest is responding physically as well as verbally to your statements and movements is important. Think of dialogue as a sport (some people take that too literally). To be comfortable and proficient in any sport one must practice, practice, practice. So have fun with reciprocal listening. You may discover that your person of interest is sitting right in front of you. It is important to remember that our perceptions may be skewed because of our heavy baggage. This is where our support system comes in to help validate what is real and what is skewed by our baggage (past history). This is where we need to listen and hear because if our baggage is weighing us down too much we will forever be stuck. We are not talking about forgetting our baggage, we are talking about realizing that baggage is just what it is— baggage. The person in front of us may not be perfect, but neither are we. The question is: Are they the perfect person for you? Check your character list.

Stop, look and listen. When you meet that person remember that you are the prize, the present to be slowly unwrapped. You are the one who is choosing. You have the power. So stop, look and listen. If that person is saying they don't want to get married, then hear it. If that person is saying they don't like to exercise, then hear it. Think of you and that person as a beautiful 1968 Camaro. You don't want to change it. It's beautiful just as it is. So when you meet that person really hear the words and see the body language to see if they are matching or if they are giving you mixed messages. If the initial meeting is questionable, perhaps the next one will assist you in making your decision. Remember the "no have to's" principle. This time will never be back. Do what flows, and have fun with it. Giving people a second chance may work for you. Remember, the person could have been nervous and may be more relaxed on a second date.

Bempathy Tip:

Communicating *a casual interest to someone is flirting which is important in* **connecting** *during the dating process and when* **committed** *to keep the relationship sizzling.*

CHAPTER 11

Laughter

How to find the humor in life? That is a question so many people would like to answer. I want to start with a short story about my morning today. Yes, today. Remember, in this book you learned that short stories help create a warm and fuzzy atmosphere and help draw people into your conversations. So here goes.

My story begins with me waking up thinking about what I was going to write in this chapter. I felt refreshed from a wonderful solid sleep and thought, *this is going to be a great day.* You've had one of those mornings. I got up, drank some aromatic coffee and did a half hour of research on the computer on "humor and laughter" and how that improves relationships. Then I packed up to leave for the hospital where I contract once a week to perform group therapy. As I was driving I was listening to a great song on the radio, "It's a Hell of a Life," thinking, *Wow, those words are thought-provoking. What a great topic to start my group with today.* The song talks about how we all are lost at times in our life and that's when we need to look at what we have and appreciate it. Then I was thinking about how to make that song humorous. All of a sudden I was going through the toll booth on Beltway 8, feeling great, singing, thinking about my book and teaching people about humor. And what do you think happened? A rock. Yes, a huge rock flew right in front of me, and being 29 years old (LOL) my reaction time isn't what it used to be. My front tire went pop! Wow, here I am believing in the law of attraction, and a rock flattens my tire. So I can't get to work. I need to find a place that has my special tire and spend money doing so. A lot of money.

Now I could have said, "That law of attraction doesn't work" and gone on to have a horrible day. Instead I said, "What's with this? I'm happy, listening to a great song, thinking about fun things and a huge rock just blew out my tire." I immediately turned on my hazard lights and tried to get over onto the shoulder (of course no one was letting me get over). The entire time I was thinking about where the humor in this was. Seriously, what could be so funny about missing work, finding a tire place, sitting for hours waiting for the tire (because they don't have it and have to call around) and then dishing out a lot of money?

All I know is that when I called to tell the story to my boss at the hospital she laughed. I told it as it happened, and I also said that I found it so weird because I believe in the law of attraction. I was happy before it happened. I asked her (she is a therapist too), "What in the heck does that mean?" Then we both laughed. Sometimes things just happen, and this was the perfect time to look for the humor in it.

The point of the story is, "Don't take yourself so seriously." Sometimes things just happen. We are in control of how we look at a situation and how we present it. The above is a perfect example of how life is humorous. That's what comedians do. Think about it. Watch any good comedy routine, and the comedian will be making fun of life situations. I am not talking about putting yourself down. I am talking about seeing the whole picture and generalizing about what is funny rather than personalizing it. Notice that I didn't focus on me and how I ran into the rock. I focused on the whole picture. You can be that person too. One day Mark Twain saw his obituary in the newspaper. During a lecture he said to his audience: "Rumors of my death have been greatly exaggerated." He looked at the humor of what was written about him. Live with laughter just as Mark Twain did. Think about the short story above and how the bullet points below apply to using humor:

- Diffuses power struggles
- Opens people up
- Energizes (laughter)
- Overcomes awkwardness
- Improves rapport
- Creates intimacy and connection
- Eases tension
- Helps to attract others
- Distracts
- Grabs attention
- Makes people look at you in a positive light
- Inspires creativity
- Lightens conversation
- Helps to change the subject

Humor is a great distraction for both you *and* people you communicate with. Several studies, including one in the *Journal of Abnormal and Social Psychology*, have shown that humor can be extremely persuasive when talking about subject matter that others may disagree with. Humor distracts people from immediately creating arguments. We all have our beliefs, perceptions and values that govern what we believe is right. Using humor diffuses the power struggle to win. Both parties are winners when they laugh, as illustrated by my story. Both my boss and I laughed. Humor makes you look more confident, positive and happy.

The big question is when to use humor. Does too much humor cause issues? Humor may be a double-edged sword. In other words, it is important to know when using humor is useful and when it is not. People want to be taken seriously, yet they also want to have fun. Before using humor it is important to ask yourself if it is:

- the appropriate time
- relevant to the topic
- offensive to the person you are talking with (sarcasm, making fun of others)

The key is to know your audience. Sit back and listen to the other person's views and their reactions to your comments. It is important not to make fun of others. That only makes you look unpleasant and insecure. Making fun of yourself (too much) may also cause issues. So what are we talking about when we are talking about humor?

What is humor? Humor is something that is amusing to both parties. Just making fun of someone, on the other hand, might sound like you are belittling them. Instead of being funny you might appear to be hurtful. Humor is considered a form of communication that we all use differently. We are all unique and think differently. Nevertheless, as humans we can bond by using humor. Humor can bring us closer together by finding commonality in ourselves and others. Humor can draw people into your conversation. No one is perfect. Most people can relate to individuals who get a kick out of their own imperfections or life's absurdities.

That improbable rock flying under my tire at a moment when I was thinking only of positive things turned out to be a great example of life's absurdities. It sure didn't fit with the law of attraction. By treating that situation with humor I was able to draw my boss in with laughter. That is what I am talking about. Studies link a sense of humor to good health. After all, how can you be anxious at the same time you are laughing? Think about it.

You don't always need other people to entertain you if you are entertained by yourself. "Sometimes you just gotta laugh." That's what I say when things may not be going my way or some person during the day may not be meeting my expectations. (My grammar may not always be the best. You might need to "adjust" that statement to say: "Sometimes you just need to laugh." Whatever works for you.)

Make up a statement that adjusts your attitude to make your day more optimistic. "Sometimes you just gotta laugh" works for me. My day ended up being a great day. I happened to have my computer with me, and I worked on this chapter as I sat and waited for my tire to be changed and my wheels to be aligned. My wallet may have felt lighter, but because of my attitude I had a day full of smiles, including my own. So think of something to say when things don't go the way you expected. Have it on hand and ready to use throughout your day.

Maybe your attitude needs an "alignment," as did my beautiful car. As you can tell by reading this book, I am really into cars. They are beautiful and can last a long time depending on the care given to them. Actually, I don't know how often a car needs an alignment. I do know that if it goes over too many bumps it needs to be adjusted so that it runs smoothly and all the wheels wear evenly. Therefore, think of changing your attitude as getting an alignment. We all have bumps during the day. That day happened to be an explosive one—for my car, that is.

Are you running over some bumps in your road to finding that perfect person for you? Does it feel like a knock, hit, blowout, collision, bang, whack, thump, fender bender or a complete pile up? If so, let's all pull back the throttle, slow down and get that alignment. It may be just the adjustment you need to have a smoother ride. The more aligned your car is, the better the ride is. Doesn't that sound like people? The more aligned we are, the better we ride through our relationships. Laughter and humor help to keep us on the right track. If you are in the midst of an argument, humor will help you to change gears to a happier topic. If the conversation is dwindling, humor may spice it up a bit. Humor relieves tension and stress, uplifts mood, increases creativity, boosts energy and brings people closer together. Wow, that sounds like a great ride to me. Do you want to come along? Let's go.

Wanting an attitude adjustment

The first part of an attitude adjustment is to be open to taking yourself with a grain of salt. In other words, don't take yourself too seriously. Everyone makes mistakes, and sometimes life is funny. It all depends on how you look at it. Yes, some things are just plain sad. We are not talking about those particular situations. We are talking about life's imperfections and life's small idiosyncrasies. Foibles sometimes just happen. Instead of letting these flaws limit you, let them draw you closer to someone who may have common foibles.

1. LAUGH AT YOURSELF

"Laugh at yourself and the world will laugh with you." If you want to feel good and exercise at the same time, laugh out loud. By the way texting "LOL" is not the same thing. Studies have found that 30 minutes of laughing has the same effect that 15 minutes of aerobics does. There are literally "laughing" support groups. You can Google them. There is even a type of yoga called Laughter Yoga. So, the next time you make a mistake work at seeing it as hilarious and learn from it.

2. PUT HUMOR IN YOUR LIFE

First and foremost, start watching comedy movies and listening to comedians (that you like). Try and do this every day for at least 15 minutes. If that's not fun for you, find something to watch that makes you laugh, or listen to humorous podcasts in your car.

3. LOOKING THROUGH THE LOOKING GLASS

If you have a "looking glass," otherwise called "a mirror" at home, then you may not need to go to any groups. Use your mirror to look at yourself and smile. If you need to take your hands and pull the two ends of your mouth up, do it.

Research has shown that smiling increases endorphins. It is even more powerful if you crinkle your eyes at the same time. Heck, while you're at it, you can tell yourself a funny joke while looking in the mirror. How do you look? Do you look tense or relaxed? Do you look like you are having fun? If not, practice until you do. When you look relaxed, other people will mirror that. Have fun with this. Make yourself crack up.

4. PRACTICE

Practice using humor in your everyday conversations. Every time you talk to friends, business acquaintances or people in general start listening and looking to see what they find humorous. Everyone is unique, yet there are some things that most people find funny:

- People intentionally tripping
- Blunders, using the wrong words (newscasters, yourself)
- Wearing two different socks
- Bloopers (the TV show)
- Sports and newscaster bloopers
- Getting a flat
- Funny vacation mishaps
- Remembering high school days, past funny times

5. BOOK OF FUNNIES

Write down things that you have done or that have happened in the past that you think are funny. When you read them they will make you laugh. These writings will not only keep your spirits up, they will also give you lots of stuff with which to spice up conversations.

Use the power of laughter to entice others and to strengthen relationships. It's important that a joke be funny to both parties to do its job of enticing and strengthening. If someone is the butt of someone's joke, then the joke will most likely be funny only to the person who tells it and not to the person it is about. Also, if the other person can't relate to the joke, then it won't be as intriguing and may even make the other person uncomfortable, especially if they think they "have to" laugh.

Humor can create a sense of connection, a positive link, between two people. Putting a humorous spin on a situation can create intimacy. For example, when lecturers give a talk, what do they often start with? Sure, a joke—to break the ice. Now, unless you are a professional comedian, I would not suggest telling a joke on the first meeting. That could increase instead of decrease awkwardness. Polite people might think they "have to" laugh at your joke, even if 1) they did not get it or 2) it was poorly told.

In order to keep the first date light and breezy you can use humor to change the subject or to lighten the intensity of the topic. For example, let's say you are talking about family, and the subject matter becomes too intense or too intimate for a first meeting. You can immediately change the subject by smiling and saying, for instance, that something about the colors of the restaurant reminds you of something funny—a duck, a walrus, a clown, a vacation, etc. There! You just lightened the conversation by relating the colors of the restaurant to something cute or funny, and the subject of the conversation has been changed.

It's easy. You know the saying that tells us to look at life through rose-colored glasses? Well, we can also look at life through humor. Now, there is a time and a place to use humor and a time and a place to be serious. If someone you just met only wants to be serious, then maybe that someone is not who you want to be with. A date is a visit, a time and a place to chat and to get to know each other. So don't try to cram a visit with too much information or too much seriousness. Life is meant to be fun. Visits are meant to be enjoyable. They're opportunities to look at the positives. Keep them short and sweet.

Imagine yourself at a party. Who do you gravitate toward? Probably the people that are laughing and having fun! The expectation for a first date is to have fun and to get to know the other person, not to marry them. What funny things can you talk about to break the ice? Be prepared so that you will have funny topics at hand. Humor will increase your self-comfort. If you are comfortable, then the person you are with will be more comfortable as well.

Some people are naturally witty and find humorous banter easy to do. Others are more serious and tend to see the logical side of life. That doesn't mean they can't put humor into their lives or conversations. The question is how to know when humor is used too much. The answer is that the conversation should flow. Sometimes when we try too hard it can cause discomfort, which can further cause the conversation to become stifled. When we push too hard we get resistance.

Humor is important. However, if you are uncomfortable with looking at the lighter side of things, then my suggestion is to practice. That's right. Baseball players, musicians, teachers and comics, among others, all need to practice to become proficient and comfortable with what they do. To become an expert at having fun or being funny you need to practice. So start having fun!

Bempathy Tip:

Humor is used to **communicate commonality connecting** *you to the other person while easing tension (increasing* **comfortability***) and creating a* **commitment** *to a conversation when done at the right time and place.*

CHAPTER 12

Know your ABCDs

Always have fun

Be busy

Consistency counts

Date

Before I go through your ABCDs, let's remember that the purpose of this book is to help you obtain an amazing relationship with a special someone. As a matter of fact, just say that out loud right now: "I am in the process of having an amazing relationship with a special someone." How did that make you feel? Perhaps you need to say it louder and look at how wonderful you look in the mirror while you say it. This chapter is the last chapter and could be the most important because it talks about your ABCDs. If we didn't learn our ABCs in elementary school, then how would we read, spell, learn and communicate? It's the same for the ABCDs of relationships. The ABCDs of relationships are: *Always have fun*; *Be busy*; *Consistency counts* and *Date*. This chapter will elaborate on these easy steps. They will help you to relish the dating world. The first of the four is:

Always have fun

Nowadays fun might be playing with our new phones, iPads, tablets and other technological devices. We seem to be finding that more fun than talking to the person beside us. Some people actually physically sit next to each other and text instead of verbally talk. Some people text while the other person just sits there which is called "phubbing." Look it up! What happened to the art of flirting? Since the beginning of time flirting has been thought of as fun. In other words, this section is about learning to have fun with whatever you are doing with people. That includes a blind date.

Recently, someone told me that before she goes on a date she recites this mantra: "This is going to go great. He is going to love me. He will love to be with me. He will date me for as long as I want." Something like that. The point is that every time she says that mantra to herself she has a fun time no matter what happens. You could make up your own mantra to make your day, date or life more fun. What is your mantra? Write it below:

_____

_____

_____

To always have fun means that you look for the fun in anything that you do. It could be work, housework, school or being with family—basically all of life. If I have a pimple in the middle of my forehead I can chose to focus on that pimple or I can choose to focus on my new outfit that fits me to a T. It's my choice. My focus will not only affect how I act and feel, it will affect who is attracted to me and what they see in me. If I focus on my pimple, I will be talking about it. If I talk about it, others will listen to what I am saying. They will most likely start focusing on my pimple too. Is that what you want? Or do you want them to focus on the spectacular you?

People are attracted to people who are having fun. People who are having fun, who look at life with humor, are usually likable, have a great social life and are seldom bored. Do you want to have fun? You can. You have the power to put humor into your life and soul. In other words, look for the excitement, pleasure and enjoyment in as many life situations as you can. Some things that happen in life just plain aren't funny. Those aren't the situations we are talking about here. We are talking about the daily life issues in our daily life routine. For example, if the dry cleaners shrunk your favorite expensive suit, laugh and make a joke of it. This could be a great story to laugh over with friends while having a drink. This is what we are talking about.

We have already touched on "attitude adjustment." This section is about being that fun person. It's about living it. In other words, it's about taking action. How do you act after doing something that you found enjoyable? Relaxed, excited, wanting more? This is what I am talking about. Don't just pretend to have fun or be funny. Live it. Be it. Be authentic.

Do more of what you find entertaining. You might want to do fun things with other people insofar as this book is about meeting people. Because we are talking about action, this would require a group of people doing activities. Some meet ups and activities were talked about in an earlier chapter. If you want, go back and look at Chapter 5 to find out what kind of activity would be fun for you. Then do more of it. "Practice makes perfect," or at least you may feel that way.

If you are shy or not outgoing, then that is who you are. It doesn't mean that you can't learn to be comfortable with people. Being with people who are doing activities takes the pressure off the need to verbally communicate. Make sure that it is an activity you like doing such as biking, painting, sculpting, a team sport, etc., so that you immediately have something in common with the others in the group. This could also be a good opportunity to observe people who are outgoing. Make it a learning experience. Practice having fun and learning at the same time. Watch how outgoing people approach others and how others react to them, and then listen to what they both say. It's almost like watching a movie that you are participating in.

While you're watching people, remember not to stare. There is a difference between observing and gawking. By putting a smile on your face you will appear to be enjoying your surroundings and enjoying what you see. No one would ever guess that you were observing them unless they have read this book. Your smile will not only make you look non-conspicuous, it will also attract people to you. Do it for fun and see what happens. Take this time to just enjoy yourself without any expectations except to learn and have fun.

Sharing a common interest will make it easier to start a conversation with someone in the group. If you were skeet shooting, you could laugh about how off you were in your skeet shooting and how glad you were that you didn't hit a bird. Asking people in your group how they like shooting would get people to talk. There you have it! You have just drawn them into you. People are easy. They just want to be heard and appreciated and to have fun.

Active people attract active people. People living up to their full potential and having fun doing it will be attracted to you. It is important to know what your skills are. You have already listed these in Chapter 4. If you are good at talking, then do things that accentuate talking such as toast mastering, speaking at engagements, teaching, or volunteering at schools. This way you are enjoying what you are doing, helping others and meeting people. Isn't that what this book is about? How easy is that??

Being around people with similar interests will make you feel more comfortable with yourself. The shared positive thoughts will radiate into the rest of your life and relationships. Hanging around people who listen, laugh and are active will help you put more enjoyment into your world. Remember, like attracts like for a reason. If you are happy, then why hang around people who are always complaining and nagging about something? You want to be with people who adore life.

The love journal

How do you feel about you and your life? What do you adore about you and the life you live? Take a moment and think. What are all your positive traits that you just love? Go to the dollar store and pick up a colorful notebook in which to write down all the positive things about you. Write in the journal only when you are feeling great about yourself. Read it when you are feeling negative about yourself or just not having a great day. That should inspire you to adore your world and attract people who feel and think the same.

How to be more fun:

1. Live dynamically
2. Live interested
3. Live spontaneously
4. Live confidently
5. Live believing
6. Live friendly
7. Live healthy
8. Live open minded
9. Live with humor
10. Live doing

Dance, sing, laugh, love and live life. Learn to appreciate each moment. Sometimes life tries us, perhaps to help us appreciate better times (that would be a positive way to look at it). Remember, everything is temporary, and a second will be gone in a second. Life is precious, and the more we appreciate what we have and who we are as human beings, the more others will do the same. You will start to exude these feelings to others. People who feel the same will gravitate toward you. Speak and do things from the heart and people will listen—at least the people you want to be with will. Listen to what the army says. "Be all you can be," and have fun with it.

Be busy

Now that you know how to have fun when doing any of your daily activities, the question is: What are you doing to keep busy? I don't mean so busy that you become stressed. Rather, I'm talking about "having a life and enjoying the moments." You have probably heard the saying, "Get a life." What does that mean to you? Well, in this section it means: Find out who you are and what you like, and go do it.

When dating or in a relationship, it is important to know that you like being with you. Whether you are busy cleaning the house, cleaning the car or going for a walk, you should be doing it with satisfaction. You need to love yourself so much that it doesn't matter what you are doing. You are enjoying your own company. You don't need anyone else to make you feel complete. This is a key realization.

We found out in the beginning of the book that you aren't broken and don't need to be fixed. You may just need an adjustment. You may just need to become more aligned with what you want and where you want to go. You are a complete person without anyone else in your life. You are looking for someone to share your completeness. When you appreciate yourself and your own time, others will do the same. If they don't, then you will know not to hang around them.

I know someone who just broke up with someone and to keep busy he went out with a different person almost every night. On the nights he didn't, he went to a party or out with friends. After a while this person got "burned out." He said, "I can't do this anymore." That is what would be considered being "too busy." When we talk about "busy" we mean doing things you enjoy and getting out of the house as much as you can without overdoing it. If it starts not to be fun, then you are overdoing it.

If you stay at home on the computer, phone, or watching TV, then most likely your special someone won't be knocking at your door unless it's the UPS person. I tell clients that to meet someone significant they first need to *be* that someone special, inside and out.

Do what you consider to be interesting activities. People like people who have interests. People like interesting people. What are your interests? What are you interested in? Do that. Don't just go out to go out. Go out to enjoy yourself and improve your life. When we do the same old thing every day it gets boring, at least for most people. Some people have the same old job doing the same old thing. They need to spice that up by incorporating other activities into their lives. Did you know that being bored can be stressful? So get interested!

When you go out and do things that interest you, you will be with other people who think the same. This is also when a good support system comes in handy to help motivate you to go out. You could call them your cheerleaders. They let you know how wonderful you are and how much fun it is to go to events that interest you.

Consistency

Consistency in a relationship and in life helps to keep things steady. This makes me think of the fable about the tortoise and the hare. Do you remember who won? That's right, the tortoise won because he was "slow and steady." His behavior was constant throughout the race whereas the rabbit who was supposed to be faster was inconsistent. So my question to you is, "Do you want to win the race to an awesome relationship?" All through this book I have been talking about pulling back the throttle and slowing your pace down a bit to enjoy the ride. Now consistency is being added to help steady the ride.

Being consistent doesn't mean that you need to be boring. To keep the spice in a relationship, spontaneity is important as well. We are talking about being consistent in your actions, your rules and where you place your boundaries. Yes, we all have our own rules. That is where the words "should" and "shouldn't" come in.

He *should* have brought me flowers. She *should* have kissed me on the first date. I *shouldn't* have said that. Believe it or not, "should" is a powerful word that may cause someone to get angry or that may even cause a fight. Think about it. How many times a day do you say it? When you do say it, how do you feel before and after? Every time you say "should" you are most likely breaking a rule of yours. Oh no! What to do? Well, for starters let's take that word out of our vocabulary, at least when talking with our future partner. When we say "should," let's listen to ourselves and remember how important this rule is to us.

You are the most important person in your world. Some may argue that. But think about it. If there is no "you," then there is no "your world." When you are sad, your world is sad and the people around you are probably miserable too. If you are happy, your world is happy (remember your first love). Your rules are therefore important, although some of your rules may need to be modified or adjusted. That's up to you to decide. So be consistent and listen to what you are "shoulding." This will help you to read yourself and will help others to read you as well.

What are your rules? I did say that we were not going to talk about any *particular* rules when meeting people. That is true. However, it is important to know what your overall governing rules are. They usually are what you value, which was touched on in Chapter 4. Your behavior should match your values, and the person you are with should know your values and visa versa. No, don't ask the person, "So what do you value?" It is best to just let things flow and to observe their behavior and listen to their words while doing the same to yourself. Listen to their "shoulds." Slowly but surely you will realize how much your values match theirs or don't. For instance, if you value time and your soon to be partner is usually late, then what does that tell you? That person may not value your time. That's what I would call a "red flag." Please don't ignore your red flags no matter how sexy the other person is. Sexy will not overrule a red flag.

It may be easier to have sex with someone than to talk intimately about "things" with them. Remember that when you meet your special someone for the first time. Be consistent with your values so that the other person will be able to read what they are and also so that you can know who you are and what you want. If you are late on some occasions and not on others, or if you go to some family functions but not to most, or if you say "should" regarding flowers on one week and not on another, then this can become confusing to the person you are with and could be considered playing games.

I hear the words "playing games" from people in the dating world more times than I care to mention. Being inconsistent promotes what I like to call the "push/pull" effect, what other people call "playing games." However, it is not so much people playing games as it is people being inconsistent with their actions and emotions that causes trouble. You may have heard it called "emotionally unavailable" or "doing a tit for a tat." Either way, it causes a tug of war. This behavior may be caused by carrying too much excess baggage from previous relationships into a new relationship or it may be caused by worry/fear about commitment and what that may bring to a person's future. People are people, and most don't want pain. Some people will do anything to avoid pain or painful situations. This causes walls to go up for protection.

Some walls are larger and thicker to break down than others. Like attracts like. Therefore, if you are with someone and you are feeling the push and pull, then please look at yourself and see what you are doing. Action creates reaction. How are you reacting to their push? To their pull? It takes two sides to play tug of war, and there is only one side that wins. Who wants to be pulled through the mud? Some people like the excitement that comes from playing tug of war. Do you?

I am here to let you know that you have choices. You can either be consistent with your boundaries and with your values or you can fluctuate (tug of war). The question is: What do you want in your relationship? How do you want it to go? Now I am not saying that things always will go your way. I would be lying if I said that. What I am saying is that if the relationship is not going the way you want and you have been authentic with your feelings, then you may want to get a second opinion from a counselor or move on. If you move on, then it's important that you learn from that experience so that it is not repeated. Ask yourself if this is the type of relationship that you have been looking for, one that makes you a better person, or if it is too "heavy" and bringing you down.

Even before the first meeting with someone, ask yourself if you are consistently answering the questions below:

1. How do I present myself?
2. What do I want to project to others?
3. What image do I want to portray (self-image)
4. Am I making people feel safe and comfortable?
5. Am I talking more of what I don't like instead of what I like?
6. What do I want the other person to focus on?

Are you consistent with your answers to the above questions? Or as consistent as can be? No one is perfect. We are talking about being dependable and trustworthy with your words and actions. Do your activities match your words and vice versa? Like attracts like. If you want someone who is loving and helpful and constructive in their communication, then ask yourself if you are being the same.

What is the message you want to send? Example: "I'm desperate" or "I'm independent and fun"?
Write the message you want to send here:

_____

_____

After writing the above, ask a friend if you are exhibiting the message you have just written.

When you begin a relationship with someone ask yourself if the relationship makes you a better you or if it drains you. Are you getting what you want from the relationship? Having a push/pull relationship can be tiring. It can sometimes feel like an anchor weighing you down. Push/pull can mean that your signals or the other person's signals are inconsistent. For instance, when someone wants to be with you a lot, you might emotionally and physically pull away—or vice versa. When you both are being consistent with your behaviors, then your relationship will be more secure. Consistency will encourage and energize the relationship because it will form reliability and predictability. If that isn't happening at the beginning of the relationship, then it might be a big red flag. You might want to talk about that with a professional. Or you might want to move on.

Yes, there may be some people who do this push/pull thing on purpose. However, those are not the people that I'm talking about. I'm talking about people who give mixed signals and wonder why they are attracting the "bad boy" or the "unavailable woman." What messages might they be giving out? People who want a committed relationship yet disrespect the other by not calling when they say they will or cancelling at the last minute for another engagement are giving either mixed signals or the wrong message.

It is important for both parties to be consistent when communicating affection, attention and appreciation. That means "routinely." The key is to hear what the other person is saying. If they are consistently saying they don't want to get married, or they don't want a committed relationship, or they don't want peanut butter, then they don't. You can't make someone like peanut butter if they don't. So don't try. Move on to someone who does. You are worth it!

Communication itself benefits from consistency. Consistently eliminating the words "why" or "you" when starting a sentence can help make your communication run smoother and more constructively. These words tend to put people on the defensive. Instead of using "why," use words such as "what," "when," "where," and "how." Instead of using "you," start out with an "I" to state how you feel. Remember while doing this that anger is a secondary emotion most likely triggered from feelings of hurt or fear. An example would be, "I feel/felt hurt when . . ." or "I feel/felt scared when . . ." This way you draw people into your conversation without putting them on the defensive and making them pull away.

Anyone can become angry. That is easy. But to be angry with the right person, to the right degree, at the right time for the right purpose and in the right way—that is not easy.

Aristotle 384 BC to 322 BC

Consistent behavior means being consistent in modeling the behavior that is wanted from someone else. Studies have shown that how people express themselves behaviorally—behaviors such as yelling or acting out—is learned and can be unlearned. Therefore, when you want someone to learn a better behavior, model it. Be consistent in your modeling behavior so that you don't confuse your receiver. A great example is "texting." If you want someone to call and not text, then model it. Yes, that's right. If a guy or gal texts you, then consistently respond with a call. You may just get them to switch from texting to calling you. If, after letting them know with "I" statements and modeling, they don't follow suit, then maybe it is time to again ask yourself what it is that you want from *your* relationship. You have choices. Is it a deal breaker, or can you live with it? If you can live with it, then go with the flow. If you cannot, then it may be good to know this at the beginning of the relationship rather than after you've gotten engaged or married.

Everyone has patterns. That doesn't mean that people can't adjust their patterns or align them with yours. Patterns are consistent behaviors that have become habitual. It is good to know the past patterns of your potential partner so that you can know what to expect. Examples of patterns are jumping from job to job or relationship to relationship, being continually late, consistently causing a mess, or yelling when angry. These are patterns. They're not necessarily deal breakers. There are no perfect people, only the perfect person for you. A person's particular patterns may be adjusted to fit well with yours.

Things do not change, we change.

Henry David Thoreau

If the relationship is flowing and you feel secure, then that is a good sign it is working for you. It is important to note that healthy relationships have arguments. It's not the arguing that is a problem.

It is 1) the way in which you argue and 2) how much you argue that may be detrimental to a relationship. Through arguments you learn. So when I speak of flow I am speaking about both parties growing and feeling fulfilled. The relationship is flowing when having this person in your life makes you the best you can be.

Date

I've saved this section for last. Having a healthy support system is quite important in contributing to help stabilize a person's life. We are social creatures, and most of us need support and comfort from others. I talked about this in Chapter 4.

Men and women both need a social life. It is essential to note that men tend not to have as big a social life as women, which is all the more reason for them to socialize. A lack of social life might be attributed to a man's desire to reduce his competition in the social environment. Having other friends in your life when dating may help balance out your focus. What that means is that if you just have one person to focus on, then you might become obsessed or consumed by that person. Having other interests in your life will ensure that you are less consumed and more balanced, which will help you make more sensible decisions.

"Date" doesn't just mean date others; it means go to social events, do collective things, collaborate with others. Which reminds me of the motto, "United we stand, divided we fall." It's a great motto. It means that we are stronger in numbers. Now, the fourth chapter talked about us being a gift and finding our independence. That remains true. Having a healthy social life or social system in place doesn't mean that we are not strong or independent. What it does mean is that it is sometimes good to have someone to lean on.

Having other interests makes you an interesting person. Two sayings are appropriate for this section: 1) People want what they can't have and 2) People appreciate what they have worked hard for.

Therefore, don't be easy. This goes for both men and women. No, this is not a game. The theme of this entire book echoes the moral of the "Tortoise and the Hare" fable. Slow and steady does it. In our society, the rarer the object is, the higher the price for it will be. It might even become priceless. Watch "Antiques Roadshow" to see what I mean. We are talking, "supply and demand."

Men and women are people and people are the same in so many ways. When I was very young my mom wrote a beautiful saying in my "autograph" book. This was a book of blank pages in which I got my friends and family to write something meaningful. My mom wrote: "Old friends are like diamonds, precious and rare; new friends are like autumn leaves found everywhere." It was so beautiful. I still remember it to this day. It means that "old friends" are precious and rare because you work hard to keep them in your life. Be that precious and rare person in your partner's life.

Work on your social system. Go to parties. Go to network groups. Volunteer and help in organizations. Join exciting activities where you can meet entertaining people and have fun.

The more pleasure you put into your life, the more exhilarating your life will be. People want to be with people who enjoy their life and live it to the fullest. This is your one life. Be that gift you wrote about in Chapter 4.

Anyone who is with you is lucky to be with you and you with them. Think of yourself and your new love as two trees growing side by side, your branches slightly touching. When the wind blows, your branches may entwine. Otherwise your branches just brush up against each other with a slight "tickle." Each of you have solid roots planted firmly in the earth and are growing straight toward the warmth of the sun. Each of you is independent and strong, able to bend and sway during a squall. Each of you wants passionately to live and grow alongside the other.

Use your ABCDs to help your relationship blossom. Men, take note that flowers might make a woman smile among other things . . . . Most important for everyone: "Enjoy!"

"Everything is relational." Have fun practicing.

Bempathy Tip:

Communicate commonality promoting **connectedness** for both parties, increasing **comfortability** so that you both will feel more in **control** promoting a **commitment** to moving into the relationships. Remember slow and easy does it. There is no rush if you are going to be with this person forever.

TM

Bempathy has three full-of-life characters as seen above. Beacon, Brighten and Bow illustrate the three personality types: a leader, a follower, and a compromiser. The fraternal twins are Beacon, who leads the way, and Brighten, who follows and is enlightened. Bow the dog helps connect the dots. In the next *Bempathy* books these characters will take you through a fictional story while relating more of these complex analytical communication techniques. They will take the difficult analytical techniques in the communication process and simplify them by looking through children's eyes.

The other Bempathy books include *Bempathy®: Looking thru Children's Eyes to Simplify Communication* which is "Available Now." *Bempathy®: Simplify Communication by Looking at the Third Side of the Coin* is coming out soon. The above characters are available for licensing; please contact us at jillrp@sbcglobal.net.

Acknowledgments

There are too many names to mention, all of whom have supported, inspired and believed in this book. My thanks to co-workers, industry professionals and to the individuals who have come to me for help. You know who you are.

Special thanks to Roger Mensink for his expert editing; to Jon Reis for his wonderful graphic cover design and to John Greenhill who with his persistence on having me write out a plan helped me to complete my goal of writing this book.

My love and gratitude to my parents, particularly for my mom's motivational notes; my brothers, especially Spencer; my son Taylor; my husband and my dear friends for their support and encouragement to write this book.

Jill Robin Payne, MA, LPC-S, LCDC, is a Licensed Professional Counselor – Supervisor and a Licensed Chemical Dependency counselor who is also Certified in Equine Assisted Psychotherapy (EAGALA).

Jill was the first student from her college to intern at the National Institutes of Health in Bethesda, Maryland. She interned at the Veterans Administration Hospital in Houston for her master's degree. While working at Bellaire Hospital in Houston she authored a guide for positive rehabilitative activities for the emotionally and physically challenged.

During her over 40 years of work experience in the mental health field, she has given numerous lectures, taught college level Behavior Modification as an adjunct professor, is an author who continues managing a diverse practice. She is heard on all social media outlets plus local and national radio and television stations commenting on the intersection of current events and social psychology.

Jill is a member of the American Counseling Association, Houston Alumnae Chapter of ZTA, Texas State Society and a lifetime member of the Houston Livestock Show and Rodeo. She holds a Bachelor of Science Degree in Recreational Therapy from Longwood University and a Master's Degree in Clinical/Counseling Psychology with honors from Houston Christian University.

Jill's practice is devoted to advancing the notion that seeking advice for mental health is as important as seeking advice for physical health. With a background in Pilates certification, reiki mastery, hypnotherapy, an undergraduate degree in recreation therapy, and a master's in psychology, she developed a concept that she copyrighted and trademarked as Bempathy® – a term she herself coined. Bempathy® represents a unique approach to communication and social skills, combining banter with empathy to build and maintain harmonious reciprocal relationships. All of Jill's work and efforts stem directly from the heart. Her passion is to 'Spread the Goodness' using the synergy of mind, body, and Bempathy®.

Jill is very versatile as a parade grand marshal and meeting a US president in the Rose Garden, to being a published author and motivational speaker. Jill works to empower individuals in the choice and meaning of their relationships through lectures in seminars and symposiums at Texas Medical Center, Ultimate Women's Expo, West Houston Medical Center, The Empowered Summit, National Conference of States Societies, Embassies and Diplomatic Corporations, United Cerebral Palsy Telethon, HARCH, Rotary, and at numerous health and civic clubs in Houston and Washington, D.C. She has contracted at pain clinics and partial hospitalization programs throughout her career as a psychotherapist to facilitate stress, pain and anger management programs, and to provide cognitive behavioral therapy.

Her newly published book, Bempathy® Looking thru Children's Eyes to Simplify Communication can be purchased on Amazon. Her next book, Bempathy® Simplify Communication by Looking at the Third Side of the Coin is coming out soon.

She resides in Houston, Texas where she maintains a private practice and lives with her husband. Her son Taylor, is doing his residency in Family Medicine.

www.jillrobinpayne.com

Inspirational Bookmarkers

What's in it for me?

Something to think about before I say or do things.

No one is perfect.

So viva my awesome imperfections!

Be the RAI (ray) of light from that lighthouse attracting all those ships.

Respectability/Authenticity/Integrity.

Stand behind "the word" by being you.

Love takes time.

It is a process.

www.ingramcontent.com/pod-product-compliance
Lightning Source LLC
Chambersburg PA
CBHW021627120626
46545CB00002B/429

* 9 7 8 1 9 6 1 6 1 3 0 0 3 *